# The Anxiety Workbook for Girls

# The Anxiety Workbook

## for girls

Proven tips to help you go from
*freakin' out* to *chillin' out*!

**Erin A. Munroe, LMHC**

Fairview Press
Minneapolis

Published by Fairview Press, 2450 Riverside Avenue, Minneapolis, Minnesota 55454. Fairview Press is a division of Fairview Health Services, a community-focused health system, affiliated with the University of Minnesota, providing a complete range of services, from the prevention of illness and injury to care for the most complex medical conditions. For a free current catalog of Fairview Press titles, please call toll-free 1-800-544-8207. Or visit our Web site at www.fairviewpress.org.

**Library of Congress Cataloging-in-Publication Data**
Munroe, Erin A.
The anxiety workbook for girls / by Erin A. Munroe.
    p. cm.
 ISBN 978-1-57749-232-0 (alk. paper)
1. Anxiety in adolescence. 2. Anxiety in adolescence—Problems, exercises, etc. 3. Teenage girls—Psychology. I. Title.
 BF724.3.A57M86 2010
 155.5'33--dc22

Printed in the United States of America
First Printing: July 2010
14  13  12  11  10     7  6  5  4  3  2  1
Book design by Ryan Scheife, Mayfly Design (www.mayflydesign.net)

**Medical Disclaimer:**
This publication is designed to provide accurate and authoritative information in regard to the subject matter covered. It is sold with the understanding that neither the author nor the publisher is engaged in the provision or practice of medical, nursing, or professional healthcare advice or services in any jurisdiction. If medical advice or other professional assistance is required, the services of a qualified and competent professional should be sought. Neither Fairview Press nor the author is responsible or liable, directly or indirectly, for any form of damages whatsoever resulting from the use (or misuse) of information contained in or implied by these documents.

This book is dedicated to all the girls out there who worry that they just aren't good enough. You are good enough, no matter what anyone else says. You are just fine and beautiful the way you are. So, be yourself, and don't worry about it!

# Contents

# Part I

## Nice (Not Really) to Meet You, Anxiety

In this section you will get to know what anxiety is, what it feels like, why it happens, and why being a teenage girl makes you a perfect target for anxiety.

# Chapter 1

## Knots in My Stomach, Trouble Falling Asleep, Nails I Can't Stop Biting— What's Up?

Have you ever wondered whether anyone else feels the way you feel, or if you're just crazy? Do you bite your nails, tap your feet, toss and turn the night away before a big test, or feel like you might faint before a big event? These could all be signs of anxiety. But what is anxiety? Well, the definition of anxiety, as found on www.merriam-webster.com/dictionary/anxiety, is:

> **1 a:** painful or apprehensive uneasiness of mind usually over an impending or anticipated ill **b:** fearful concern or interest **c:** a cause of anxiety

> **2** an abnormal and overwhelming sense of apprehension and fear often marked by physiological signs (as sweating, tension, and increased pulse), by doubt concerning the reality and nature of the threat, and by self-doubt about one's capacity to cope with it

These are solid definitions. Many people, however, define anxiety a little differently, and most people experience anxiety in different ways. For example, some people say they feel "anxious" when they are excited about something or eager for something to happen. Have you ever had a big event in your life coming up about which you were so excited you couldn't sleep or stop thinking about it? Some people would label this feeling as anxiety, even though it has nothing to do with fear or pain. This kind of anxiety is "fun anxiety," and it's not necessarily the kind that will disrupt your life in a negative way.

The anxiety that this workbook discusses is the kind that causes stress and unsettling physical feelings—it isn't pleasant, it isn't fun, and it affects you in ways that make you uncomfortable. You might think of it as something other than anxiety—stressing out, freaking out, feeling nervous, panicking, being frazzled, worried, flipped out, under pressure, and so on. Anxiety has many names and affects all of us at some point, but some of us at many points.

How do people experience anxiety? Some people only have anxiety in certain situations, like before a test, when thinking about speaking in public, or during a social event. Others feel anxious out of the blue and aren't really sure when it will hit. And still others feel some anxiety all the time. Anxiety can be tricky; not everyone has the same physical experience, and some people might not even recognize that certain feelings are signs of their anxiety.

Here are some ways that people experience anxiety:

- Sweating
- Trouble breathing
- Butterflies in your stomach
- Feeling sick to your stomach
- Shaking
- Feeling fidgety
- Having trouble sleeping
- Numbness or tingling in parts of your body
- Sensation of chills
- Irritability/short temper
- Having trouble eating
- Having difficulty focusing
- Finding it difficult to remember things
- Feeling as though you are in a tunnel
- Feeling faint
- Feeling itchy in your own skin
- Being fearful

And some people often have habits that go along with their feelings of anxiety, such as:

- Twirling or twisting their hair
- Nail biting

- Tapping their feet
- Rocking back and forth
- Humming
- Pacing
- Pulling their hair
- Picking at their skin
- Eating more than usual even if they aren't hungry
- Chewing their pens or pencils

These are just a few of the habits that might result from anxiety. You might have anxiety and be able to list a whole lot of different feelings and habits. The funny thing is you might not even recognize your anxious habits until you look at lists like the two above and do some self-observation. In the next few activities, you will describe your own anxiety and how you react to your anxiety, figure out what causes your anxiety and when it occurs, and explore who in your family (biological and otherwise) also might have anxiety.

## Describe How You Feel Anxiety

List adjectives and feelings that you associate with your own anxiety. For example, maybe you feel crummy, self-conscious, or like you are losing your @#$*. Write it down. No one else has to see it—just you! Fill in as many lines as you like and add more if you need to; there are no right or wrong answers here.

_____    _____    _____

_____    _____    _____

_____    _____    _____

_____    _____    _____

## How Does My Anxiety Express Itself?

Think about when you feel anxious. Is there anything you habitually do? It doesn't have to be a big thing; it could be something as small as making sure you have your favorite bracelet on when you have a tough test to take, or something bigger like recognizing you have no fingernails because you chewed them up. Maybe you haven't noticed anything. Ask someone close to you: "Do I ever do anything when I seem nervous?" The answer might surprise you!

Write it down, again, for your own information:

When I feel nervous, I _____

_____

_____ .

When others think I am nervous, they say that I _____

_____

_____ .

## Where on Earth Did My Anxiety Come From?

Was I born with it? Did I get it from my family? Is it related to specific situations, people, or places? How did I end up with anxiety? Anxiety can come from a bunch of different places. If there are people in your family with anxiety, your anxiety could be passed down from them and have a genetic connection. If you were raised by someone or frequently around someone with anxiety, you could have learned to be anxious. Have you ever had a bad experience? Maybe you were stuck in an elevator and, now, when you ride in an elevator, you cringe, or your heart beats faster until the doors open and you can get out. Anxiety can develop just about anywhere. Some people seem to be more affected than others, and that seems to be simply due to differences in personality.

## Family Anxiety Quiz

1. Has anyone in your family seemed anxious to you?

   **YES** | **NO**

2. Has anyone in your family talked about being anxious?

   **YES** | **NO**

3. Has anyone in your family taken medication for anxiety?

   **YES** | **NO**

4. Has anyone in your family seen a counselor for anxiety?

   **YES** | **NO**

If you answered yes to even one of these questions, it is likely that someone in your family deals with anxiety and might understand what you are going through.

If you answered yes to two of these questions, someone in your family is definitely familiar with anxiety.

If you answered yes to three or four of these questions, not only is someone in your family anxious, but he or she also is getting help for anxiety and that is great. This person might be a good resource for you when you have questions or concerns about your own anxiety.

## What Kind of Anxiety Bothers Me?

*(Circle the letter for the answer that best describes you.)*

1. You have plans to go out with a few friends on Friday night. One friend calls and tells you a group of kids you don't know well will be coming along. You think:

   **A** Great! The more the merrier!

   **B** Whatever.

   **C** I think I might have something else to do that night; in fact, I feel ill already.

2. You have plans to go to a big party and are superexcited. As the time of the party approaches, you find yourself:

   **A** More excited than ever to go.

   **B** Feeling pretty much the same as always.

   **C** Trying to figure out which excuse not to go sounds most believable.

3. You have a presentation to do in class; you have practiced and are prepared. It is on a subject you know well. You are thinking:

   **A** Sweet—now everyone will know I am a smarty-pants.

   **B** Another day, another assignment.

   **C** I wonder if my teacher would believe that I lost my voice and can't speak for a month . . . there must be some way out of this.

4. Your new English teacher loves to call on each student at least once a day. When she looks your way, you think:

   **A** I am going to knock her socks off with my answer.

   **B** Oh good! Once I answer this question, I can go back to doodling.

   **C** Oh no oh no oh no! I might throw up.

5. Report cards are coming out at the end of the week. Your math teacher tells you your average was an 89, so he had to give you a B+ instead of the A- you were hoping for. You:

   **A** Decide he's being persnickety about grades, and will show him next term when you dazzle him with work worthy of an A.

   **B** Feel a little disappointed; you tried your hardest and got close to an A, but a B+ is darn good!

   **C** Try really hard not to cry or scream in the middle of the classroom. Once you leave class, the B+ is all you can think about. What could you have done differently? Why are you so lazy? You should have done better. You stink!

6. The results from the state science exam are back. Jenny, who is supercompetitive, got one point higher than you. You think:

   **A** Well, I did better than she did on French! Next year, look out, Jenny; I'll school *you* in science!

**B**   Cool; Jenny studies really hard and so do I. It's kind of fun to have some friendly competition.

**C**   OMG, I can't believe it—yet another person who is smarter than I am. Why do I bother? I'm obviously an idiot who completely stinks at science.

7.   You are out with friends at a sub shop after school. You look at the menu and think:

**A**   It all looks great. *Mmm.*

**B**   It is close to dinner. Maybe Cindy will split a sub with me?

**C**   What should I get? If I get a sub, it might be awkward to eat and eating in front of Joey makes me nervous. Maybe I should just get a salad or a bag of chips. They aren't sloppy to eat...

8.   It is the state finals in hockey. You are the goalie. You realize right before you step on the ice that you forgot your lucky mouth guard. You think:

**A**   I love that mouth guard!!! No time to worry about it, though. I'll have to use my practice one and get out there and win the game!

**B**   What a bummer. New mouth guards are annoying and cut my gums. Oh well. I suppose it's better to have one in than get hit in the mouth with a puck.

**C**   Oh no. We are going to lose and it'll be all my fault. I'm such an idiot. I can't even play without that mouth guard. How much time until we start? I wonder if I can get ahold of my brother to go get it and bring it here ASAP.

9.   You are at an end-of-the-school-year party and you notice that you have the same outfit on as one of the most popular girls in class. You think:

**A**   Great minds think alike! Clearly you know style when you see it!

**B**   This is a little awkward, but it's neat that we have similar tastes! I wonder if she got it on sale too?

**C**   Think? You don't think. You run. You hide. Obviously she's going to look better in it than you, so you need to change or leave the party as soon as possible.

10. You don't feel so hot after gym class. Your stomach is in turmoil. You definitely need to go to the bathroom. You:

   **A**  Find the closest bathroom available; sorry, everyone, but things might get a little stinky!

   **B**  Hurry to the nurse and tell her you don't feel well and need to use her bathroom. At least there is a little more privacy in there, and you won't stink up the big bathroom for the rest of the day.

   **C**  Run into the closest bathroom in a panic. A few girls from class are in there; what can you do? You can't hold it but you don't want them to hear you. Oh no. You turn and run to the next bathroom, hoping there is no one in there, but you see someone walk in. On the verge of tears and going to the bathroom in your pants, you run to the nurse, mortified to tell her you are sick, but you have to go somewhere.

## Answer Key

In terms of overall anxiety, if you answered mostly:

**As:** Good for you! You have some serious confidence. You might be a little competitive at times, but it seems to encourage you, not stress you out.

**Bs:** You are cool and calm as a cucumber. You try hard, appreciate others who try hard, and are pretty balanced about your decision making.

**Cs:** Whoa! Do you sleep? Looks like you have some anxiety that is making life not so much fun and causing you to beat up on your self-esteem. Let's fix that and take some tips from the As and Bs.

If you have a mixture of As, Bs, and Cs, you may have some anxieties in certain areas and none in others. Let's see what each answer might indicate:

If you answered "C" to any or all of questions 1, 2, 4, 7, or 9, it sounds like you have some social anxiety. Certain social situations may make you anxious, and make you change how you act.

If you answered "C" to any or all of questions 3, 4, 5, 6, or 8, you might struggle with performance anxiety. School, sports, and/or extracurricular performance may make you stress out!

If you answered "C" to any or all of questions 7, 9, or 10, your body seems to freak you out a bit. Self-conscious feelings seem to get in the way of how you make decisions.

What to do with the results: DON'T STRESS OUT. Seriously, this is actually for fun. Now you have a better idea of what makes you anxious and maybe you can even chuckle at it a little or see that being able to answer "a" or "b" to some of these questions would really decrease your stress level. Once we do a little more investigating, we will work on decreasing your anxiety and building up your self-esteem.

## The Family Tree of Anxiety

Let's see who else in your family has anxiety. We are going to look at your biological family as well as people who aren't blood relatives, but whom you consider close enough to be related. Since some anxiety is learned, it is important to look around at those who aren't related but might have a strong influence on how you act.

For this activity, you will need four different colored markers and potentially a family member you can ask for some family history.

1. Let's figure out whom you want to include in this family tree. Pick one color to represent biological family members. Write down the names of those in your immediate biological family—living or deceased—in this color. If you aren't living with your biological family, but you know some background on your biological family, write those names here:

    Biological mother: _____

    Biological father: _____

Biological siblings: _____

_____   _____

_____   _____

Biological grandparents:

_____   _____

_____   _____

Biological aunts and uncles: _____

_____   _____

_____   _____

_____   _____

Other biological relatives with whom you spend a good amount of time, or consider particularly close:

_____   _____

_____   _____

_____   _____

_____   _____

Now, using another color, write down the names of people you think of as your family but who are not biologically related to you. This could include an aunt who married into the family (your biological uncle's wife), a guardian, an adoptive or foster parent, your best friend, your best friend's father, a babysitter, a coach, and so on. Think of people you spend time with, or wish you spent more time with; these people tend to influence your life.

| | |
|---|---|
| _____ | _____ |
| _____ | _____ |
| _____ | _____ |
| _____ | _____ |

2. Let's see who you *suspect* has anxiety. Take a third color and circle those in your family (biological and otherwise) with this color.

3. Using the fourth color, circle the people you know for sure have anxiety—either because they have told you or a family member has confirmed it. Some family members might be circled twice. If you are comfortable doing so, check with a family member about any family history of anxiety. You might find that you have some relatives with anxiety that you never even knew had anxiety.

4. Take the names of people you circled twice and write their names here in their original color:

| | |
|---|---|
| _____ | _____ |
| _____ | _____ |
| _____ | _____ |

5. Take the names of people you circled once and write their names in their original color:

_____    _____

_____    _____

Look at the names in steps 4 and 5. Those who are biologically related to you and anxious might have given you a double whammy of anxiety by passing down a genetic predisposition and by spending time with you!

You might have learned anxious behaviors from those who are not biologically related to you but are influential in your life.

You might not have recognized some of your family members as having anxieties. Take a look at who these family members are; they might know a thing or two about managing anxiety and could be key people who could help you deal with your own anxieties.

6. You are going to gather information to see where your similarities lie with those in your family. One note of caution, however: anxiety can be difficult for many people to talk about, so if you don't think some people will be comfortable answering questions, or if they tell you they don't feel like talking about it, respect their space and move on to someone else.

If you can, interview everyone who has one or two circles around their names and ask them the following questions:

   1. Do you consider yourself anxious?
   2. At what age did you realize you had anxiety?
   3. Are you anxious about everything or just about specific things? For instance, do you feel like you worry all the time or do you only worry about flying, social situations, tests, and so on?
   4. What happens to you physically when you feel anxious? Does your heartbeat speed up? Do you sweat?
   5. Have you found anything that helps with your anxiety? If so, what?

Check out the answers you get. Some of your family members might feel just like you, and some might have some helpful suggestions for dealing with anxiety. However, if anyone recommends substance use or anything dangerous or illegal as a way to manage anxiety, say "No thanks" and move on. There are plenty of ways to deal with anxiety that do not involve substance use or danger!

## Your Weekly Anxiety Chart

We are going to call this your WACee (pronounced "wacky") Chart. That way, if you carry it around with you, no one will know what it means. If you tell them it is your wacky chart, hopefully they will be confused enough to stick to minding their own business. And if you think of it as your wacky chart, chances are it will make you giggle a bit at your behaviors and loosen up a little about your anxiety. Everyone has wacky behaviors—EVERYONE—and those behaviors are what make people individuals. When the behaviors get out of our control and have a negative effect on our lives, it is time to take a look at them and figure out how to deal with them.

For this chart, you will rate your anxiety every day for a week and see how it coincides with times of the day and activities coming up or those that have recently occurred. You will also try to mark anxious behaviors you notice about yourself. You will check in with yourself three times a day: once when you wake up, once immediately after school or around two or three o'clock in the afternoon if you aren't in school, and once before bedtime.

1. Take an inventory of how you are feeling and any behaviors you are noticing and write these down. Did you find you were anxious at all prior to this check-in? If so, write down those feelings and behaviors. Are you feeling overwhelmed and noticing that you are pacing? Are you feeling like you can't breathe and are getting irritable with people?

2. Rate your anxiety on a scale of 1 to 10, with 1 being a tiny bit nervous, but not something you are thinking about or worrying about. A 5 would be nervous or stressed, but feeling as though you have your stress or anxiety under control. Anything past 5 means you are beginning to feel like the anxiety is making your life more difficult. For example, a 7 might indicate that you have a test that you are so stressed out about that you are extra fidgety and can't concentrate on your other classes. A 10 would mean that you are so anxious about the test that you can't focus on it. Perhaps you

find that you are crying or unable to sleep, and your anxiety is ruining your ability to take the test.

3. What's coming up in the near future that could be causing anxiety? Did anything happen in the immediate past that left you feeling anxious? Did something set you off, or are you worrying about an upcoming event? Try to figure out if there is a cause. You might not be able to find one; that is okay. If it comes out of the blue, you might at least be able to find a pattern.

4. Where were you when you felt most anxious today? Were you with other people or alone? Write down who you were with and what the situation was like.

5. Was there anything that made you feel better or helped alleviate your anxiety?

Here is a sample of what the chart might look like filled out for a day.

# WACee Chart—Sample

## Day 1
## Good Morning

| Feelings | Behaviors | Scale of 1–10 | What might I be nervous about? | Where was I when I felt the most anxious/ who was I with? | Did anything make me feel better? |
|----------|-----------|---------------|-------------------------------|---------------------------------------------------------|-----------------------------------|
| Exhausted | Hid under pillow | 5 | Presentation in English | In bed! I didn't sleep and was anxious all night | My dog came to cuddle |
| Butterflies in stomach | Procrastinated getting out of bed | | | | |

## Day 1
## Afternoon

| Feelings | Behaviors | Scale of 1–10 | What might I be nervous about? | Where was I when I felt the most anxious/ who was I with? | Did anything make me feel better? |
|---|---|---|---|---|---|
| Sick to my stomach | Couldn't eat at lunch | 8 | Presentation is right after lunch | Everywhere I went! | NO |
| Angry, fidgety | Short tempered with my friends | | My presentation—I need to go over it again, but my friends keep talking to me! | Lunch with my friends | I was pretty annoyed, but my best friend did make me laugh a little, which felt good |

## Day 1
## Evening/Before Bed

| Feelings | Behaviors | Scale of 1–10 | What might I be nervous about? | Where was I when I felt the most anxious/ who was I with? | Did anything make me feel better? |
|---|---|---|---|---|---|
| A few butterflies still in my stomach | Picky about dinner, but able to eat | 4 | Presentation went well but now I am nervous about what my grade might be | Right before my presentation; once I got home I felt better | Petting my dog |
| Tired and cranky | Irritable with my little sister | | My grade, and I think I am tired from being so anxious all day | | My little sister tried to cheer me up |

## Day 1
### Good Morning

| Feelings | Behaviors | Scale of 1–10 | What might I be nervous about? | Where was I when I felt the most anxious/ who was I with? | Did anything make me feel better? |
|---|---|---|---|---|---|
|  |  |  |  |  |  |
|  |  |  |  |  |  |

## Day 1
### Afternoon

| Feelings | Behaviors | Scale of 1–10 | What might I be nervous about? | Where was I when I felt the most anxious/ who was I with? | Did anything make me feel better? |
|---|---|---|---|---|---|
|  |  |  |  |  |  |
|  |  |  |  |  |  |

## Day 1
### Evening/Before Bed

| Feelings | Behaviors | Scale of 1–10 | What might I be nervous about? | Where was I when I felt the most anxious/ who was I with? | Did anything make me feel better? |
|---|---|---|---|---|---|
|  |  |  |  |  |  |
|  |  |  |  |  |  |

## Day 2
### Good Morning

| Feelings | Behaviors | Scale of 1–10 | What might I be nervous about? | Where was I when I felt the most anxious/ who was I with? | Did anything make me feel better? |
|---|---|---|---|---|---|
|  |  |  |  |  |  |
|  |  |  |  |  |  |

## Day 2
### Afternoon

| Feelings | Behaviors | Scale of 1–10 | What might I be nervous about? | Where was I when I felt the most anxious/ who was I with? | Did anything make me feel better? |
|---|---|---|---|---|---|
|  |  |  |  |  |  |
|  |  |  |  |  |  |

## Day 2
### Evening/Before Bed

| Feelings | Behaviors | Scale of 1–10 | What might I be nervous about? | Where was I when I felt the most anxious/ who was I with? | Did anything make me feel better? |
|---|---|---|---|---|---|
|  |  |  |  |  |  |
|  |  |  |  |  |  |

## Day 3
### Good Morning

| Feelings | Behaviors | Scale of 1–10 | What might I be nervous about? | Where was I when I felt the most anxious/ who was I with? | Did anything make me feel better? |
|---|---|---|---|---|---|
|  |  |  |  |  |  |
|  |  |  |  |  |  |

## Day 3
### Afternoon

| Feelings | Behaviors | Scale of 1–10 | What might I be nervous about? | Where was I when I felt the most anxious/ who was I with? | Did anything make me feel better? |
|---|---|---|---|---|---|
|  |  |  |  |  |  |
|  |  |  |  |  |  |

## Day 3
### Evening/Before Bed

| Feelings | Behaviors | Scale of 1–10 | What might I be nervous about? | Where was I when I felt the most anxious/ who was I with? | Did anything make me feel better? |
|---|---|---|---|---|---|
|  |  |  |  |  |  |
|  |  |  |  |  |  |

## Day 4
Good Morning

| Feelings | Behaviors | Scale of 1–10 | What might I be nervous about? | Where was I when I felt the most anxious/ who was I with? | Did anything make me feel better? |
|---|---|---|---|---|---|
|  |  |  |  |  |  |
|  |  |  |  |  |  |

## Day 4
Afternoon

| Feelings | Behaviors | Scale of 1–10 | What might I be nervous about? | Where was I when I felt the most anxious/ who was I with? | Did anything make me feel better? |
|---|---|---|---|---|---|
|  |  |  |  |  |  |
|  |  |  |  |  |  |

## Day 4
Evening/Before Bed

| Feelings | Behaviors | Scale of 1–10 | What might I be nervous about? | Where was I when I felt the most anxious/ who was I with? | Did anything make me feel better? |
|---|---|---|---|---|---|
|  |  |  |  |  |  |
|  |  |  |  |  |  |

## Day 5
Good Morning

| Feelings | Behaviors | Scale of 1–10 | What might I be nervous about? | Where was I when I felt the most anxious/ who was I with? | Did anything make me feel better? |
|---|---|---|---|---|---|
| | | | | | |
| | | | | | |

## Day 5
Afternoon

| Feelings | Behaviors | Scale of 1–10 | What might I be nervous about? | Where was I when I felt the most anxious/ who was I with? | Did anything make me feel better? |
|---|---|---|---|---|---|
| | | | | | |
| | | | | | |

## Day 5
Evening/Before Bed

| Feelings | Behaviors | Scale of 1–10 | What might I be nervous about? | Where was I when I felt the most anxious/ who was I with? | Did anything make me feel better? |
|---|---|---|---|---|---|
| | | | | | |
| | | | | | |

## Day 6
### Good Morning

| Feelings | Behaviors | Scale of 1–10 | What might I be nervous about? | Where was I when I felt the most anxious/ who was I with? | Did anything make me feel better? |
|---|---|---|---|---|---|
|  |  |  |  |  |  |
|  |  |  |  |  |  |

## Day 6
### Afternoon

| Feelings | Behaviors | Scale of 1–10 | What might I be nervous about? | Where was I when I felt the most anxious/ who was I with? | Did anything make me feel better? |
|---|---|---|---|---|---|
|  |  |  |  |  |  |
|  |  |  |  |  |  |

## Day 6
### Evening/Before Bed

| Feelings | Behaviors | Scale of 1–10 | What might I be nervous about? | Where was I when I felt the most anxious/ who was I with? | Did anything make me feel better? |
|---|---|---|---|---|---|
|  |  |  |  |  |  |
|  |  |  |  |  |  |

## Day 7
Good Morning

| Feelings | Behaviors | Scale of 1–10 | What might I be nervous about? | Where was I when I felt the most anxious/ who was I with? | Did anything make me feel better? |
|---|---|---|---|---|---|
|  |  |  |  |  |  |
|  |  |  |  |  |  |

## Day 7
Afternoon

| Feelings | Behaviors | Scale of 1–10 | What might I be nervous about? | Where was I when I felt the most anxious/ who was I with? | Did anything make me feel better? |
|---|---|---|---|---|---|
|  |  |  |  |  |  |
|  |  |  |  |  |  |

## Day 7
Evening/Before Bed

| Feelings | Behaviors | Scale of 1–10 | What might I be nervous about? | Where was I when I felt the most anxious/ who was I with? | Did anything make me feel better? |
|---|---|---|---|---|---|
|  |  |  |  |  |  |
|  |  |  |  |  |  |

# Chapter 2

## Anxiety Rocks!
## (Okay, Not All the Time — but Sometimes)

Believe it or not, although anxiety can cause sweating, trouble breathing, and panic attacks, anxiety can be beneficial in some instances. The type of anxiety that negatively affects how you go about your day and live your life is considered unhealthy anxiety. Unhealthy anxiety is the kind we are going to work on, but it is important to recognize that some anxiety works for us in a healthy way. Anxiety is healthy, for example, when it motivates us to study for a test, keeps us alert while playing sports, or reminds us to be aware of our surroundings in an unfamiliar place. Without anxiety, people might lack motivation. What if you had no anxiety? If everything just rolled off your shoulders, would you be a strong competitor? Would you achieve the grades you want to achieve? Maybe not.

To understand the difference between healthy and unhealthy anxiety, it helps to know a bit about the math and science of anxiety. If math and science are not your strong points, don't worry; this is interesting and can help you better understand why your body responds the way it does in certain situations.

The math portion of anxiety is about finding a balance with respect to anxiety. If we have too little anxiety, we aren't going to have sufficient drive, motivation, or concentration. But if we have too much, we won't be sufficiently motivated because fear stands in our way. Our concentration is off because our stress is too high, and our minds will be in overdrive. Here is how this will look on a graph:

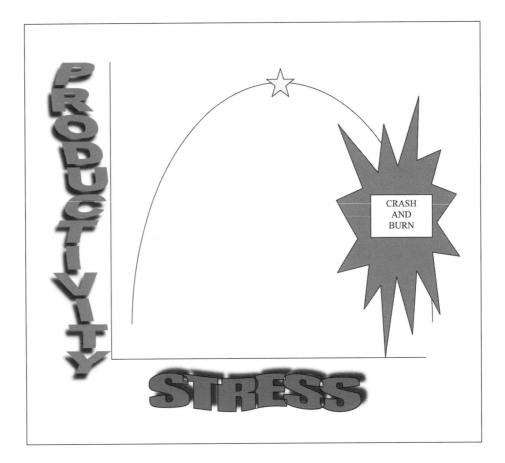

As you can see from the diagram, low stress doesn't stimulate us enough to enhance our productivity. On the other hand, too much stress causes anxiety and impairment in functioning. Somewhere in the middle seems to be where we are our sharpest, most creative, and most productive (for more on the topic of stress, go to www.mindtools.com/stress/UnderstandStress/StressPerformance.htm). So where's the middle? That is the tricky question. Everyone seems to have a different level of tolerance for stress. Some people thrive under a great deal of stress, but others just about fall apart when the tiniest amount of pressure is applied. Different amounts of stress can affect us differently in different situations. You could do fine under pressure at a spelling bee, but feel like you are going to pass out at the thought of a soccer game in gym class. The key is to figure out your anxiety threshold. To find this out, you have to get to know your anxiety and how it affects your body. In Chapter 1, you charted your feelings and behaviors in relation to your anxiety. These feelings and behaviors are big clues to figuring out when your anxiety is heightening and when you need to take action. Look back at your WACee Chart and review your behaviors and feelings. Look out for these the next time you have a project or a potentially stressful situation. Once these things start happening, it is time to rein in your anxiety—which we will get to soon.

For now, we are going to look at when anxiety is beneficial. This will help you recognize when anxiety rocks and works in your favor.

Before we get to work, there is one more important piece of the anxiety puzzle to fill in, and this is where it gets a little scientific. Not only can anxiety help you perform, it also can save your life. Sound backward? The anxiety that makes you feel as though you can't breathe might actually keep you breathing. Years ago, before schools, office jobs, civilization as we know it, we were out there with the rest of the animal kingdom, hunting prey, hiding from predators, and trying to survive. We, along with other animals, have a lifesaving response known as the "fight or flight response." This response is innate and cues us whether to stay and fight or run. Our bodies go through amazing changes when we are faced with danger; our pupils dilate so that we can take in more information; our hair does actually stand on end (the hair on your head is probably too long to stick up straight, although you might notice your arm hair getting prickly); our hearts pump harder; our lungs open up so that we can breathe better; our endorphins kick in to help us not feel pain; and we start sweating to cool off. These are only a few of the things that happen when our bodies sense danger. All of these physiological changes are lifesaving changes when we are truly threatened. If you are in danger, these changes will allow you to run fast, potentially twist an ankle but have the ability to keep running, breathe better, and so on. Anxiety rocks!

But there is a downside to this response too. Our bodies are so efficient that sensing danger can start the fight-or-flight response when we don't need it. If you have certain anxieties that you perceive as "danger," your fight-or-flight response could kick in when you can't use it. For example, if you feel these physical changes occur right before your history midterm, you better not run out of the classroom like it is on fire. That won't help your history grade. Knowing this, you sit with all these physical changes and don't use the chemicals (like the endorphins) in your body like you would if you were running from a bear. That means your body is all revved up with nowhere to go, and all this stress and energy sit inside you and can make you feel pretty icky. As we deal more with the negative effects of anxiety, we will discover fun and healthy ways of getting rid of this extra energy. For now, however, use the following activities to look at where and when anxiety has rocked your world.

### When Has Anxiety Helped You?

Using your WACee Chart from Chapter 1, find times in your week when anxiety might have helped you accomplish something. For example, take a look at the sample chart for Day 1:

# WACee Chart—Sample

## Day 1
## Good Morning

| Feelings | Behaviors | Scale of 1–10 | What might I be nervous about? | Where was I when I felt the most anxious/ who was I with? | Did anything make me feel better? |
|---|---|---|---|---|---|
| Exhausted | Hid under pillow | 5 | Presentation in English | In bed! I didn't sleep and was anxious all night | My dog came to cuddle |
| Butterflies in stomach | Procrastinated getting out of bed | | | | |

What was good about that day? It doesn't look like much, but think about how you prepared for your presentation. Did you write notes? Study hard? That was your anxiety helping you. Unfortunately, then you weren't able to sleep, which means that after preparing for your presentation, you continued to feel anxious and that anxiety caused you to stay awake. If only you could have used the positive anxiety to study and then figured out how to relax so you could sleep at night!

Look back at your week and figure out when your anxiety went haywire. Was it helping you at first? Did it then get the better of you?

Write down when your anxiety helped you throughout the week and where it seemed to turn into unhealthy anxiety.

**Example:**

*My anxiety about my grades helped motivate me to go to the library for an extra hour, but I still felt like I didn't study enough. So I stayed up all night and now I am too tired to focus on the test.*

*My anxiety about enclosed spaces led me to check out the exits in case of an emergency. I would have been prepared in case something had happened, but then I kept worrying that something would go wrong!*

When did my anxiety help me?_____

_____

_____

_____

## Do You Ever Depend on Your Anxiety?

Believe it or not, you might get something out of your anxiety that you don't really want to give up. Do you ever get special treatment because of your anxiety? For example, do you get to sit in a separate room for taking tests? Do people take care of you more when you tell them you are feeling anxious? These are considered "secondary gains" and can make it tough to give up anxiety—especially if the secondary gains are so great you would rather stay anxious than lose the benefits you get from being anxious.

Here are examples of secondary gains:

- *My mother makes my favorite foods when she knows I have a big test coming up.*
- *My math teacher lets me sit in a room by myself to take tests because of my anxiety.*
- *My teachers know I care about my grades if they see me stressing out and I talk about how stressed I am.*
- *My friends are nicer to me when I am stressed out about something because they feel bad for me.*
- *My little brother will do my chores when I seem stressed out.*

It is tough to give up secondary gains—especially if you have people showing you how much they care and helping you do things that you don't necessarily want to do. In order to help you get rid of the need for secondary gains, you need to recognize what these gains are.

Think of five secondary gains you have gotten from your anxiety and write them down:

1. _____

2. _____

3. _____

4. _____

5. _____

Could you live without these? Are there any you could get without using anxiety? If your brother does your chores when you are anxious, is there a more balanced way to work with him to help you when you are studying for a test or preparing for something stressful? Maybe if he does your chores during your stressful week you could do his chores the next week? It might sound much better to just let him do them, but by taking responsibility for what you need to get done, you will probably feel a lot better—and your brother will feel appreciated.

 ## Peace Out, Anxiety!

Have you ever written a "Dear John" letter? That is a letter you write to break up with someone. It usually goes like this:

> *Dear John,*
>
> *You are a wonderful guy, but I just don't see this working*—and so on and so forth.

Instead of writing a letter to John, you are going to write a letter to your anxiety, saying good-bye, take a hike, get lost. Don't be too cruel—point out in your letter how your anxiety has helped you out, but also why at times it is too much for you to take and gets in the way of your life.

Using the activities you have done so far, pick out the positive and negative aspects of your anxiety and wave good-bye to the parts that hinder your daily life. If you want, give your anxiety a fun name like "Stress Jess" or "Panic Paul."

**Sample:**

*Dear Anxious Andy,*

*Although I appreciate all the times you have motivated me and helped me get my work done and in on time, I really can't take the panic attacks every time I am in an elevator, or the sweaty armpits whenever I see a math test. I also hate the way you make me lose sleep, eat when I am not hungry, and get snippy with my friends. I like my friends, and they are more helpful than you!! I am kicking you to the curb. But I will take a little of you with me always—like your help in making me focus and, of course, that fight-or-flight response in case I ever need it!*

*See ya!*

Have fun with this! Be goofy or serious; it is up to you. No one ever has to see it!

Dear _____,

_____

_____

_____

_____

_____

_____

_____

# Chapter 3

## Girls Rule—As Far As Anxiety Goes

Girls rule in many areas, and one of these happens to be anxiety. Studies show that females are more prone to anxiety, but the reasons behind this are not completely clear. It could be that we are stronger and take on more stress, thus creating anxiety. It might also be that we are born with a predisposition to anxiety. Or possibly, anxiety is part of a girl's expected social role: women are expected to be anxious and therefore become anxious. There are quite a few theories out there, as well as statistics, that show that women are identified with anxiety more frequently than men.

According to research from Harvard Medical School:

*Women are twice as likely to suffer from panic disorder or social phobia compared with men, and they are three times as likely to have agoraphobia (fear of being in public places). They also face a slightly higher risk for specific phobia (fear of a particular object or situation). About 10%–14% of women will have post-traumatic stress disorder (PTSD) in their lives, compared with 5%–6% of men. And 6.6% of women will have generalized anxiety disorder, but just 3.6% of men will. (www.newswise.com/articles/view/524055)*

This is totally not fair! PTSD, panic, agoraphobia—these are probably not words you want to hear. Brilliant, fabulous, and fun would be a lot better! The good thing about these statistics, however, is that they mean you are not alone. Many other women also struggle with anxiety. Although the numbers might be smaller for men, anxiety is still something that many men also face in their lifetimes. If you can find a silver lining in anxiety, you will be able to find it just about anywhere.

So why do women seem to attract anxiety? It could be because of our ravishing good looks and stunning intellect, our wonderful teenage years, or it might be one of many theories that researchers are still studying.

If you think about yourself as a preteen and a teenager, do you or did you have any anxieties that are specific to being female? Boobs? Getting your period? Having sex? Trying to look like a completely unrealistic, totally airbrushed supermodel or actress who not only gets paid to look unlike any normal person but also employs her own personal trainer, makeup artist, hair stylist, clothing stylist, personal chef, publicist, and so on? Well, these things alone are stressful enough to cause anxiety. Are your boobs too big? Do your classmates stare at them and call you awful names or spread rumors about your sexual behavior simply because of your boobs? Do you have no boobs whatsoever and hear similar kinds of cruel things said about you, except the extreme opposite? What about your period? Did you get it early, or late? Do you have a really heavy one that makes you double over in pain? Are you supposed to have sex now, or later? Sex is a guy problem too, but there seems to be more social pressure on girls to remain pure, yet at the same time act like wild women in bed who know all sorts of tricks like the girls allude to in many popular songs. Then there is your appearance that, along with boobs, includes totally unrealistic images of women in the media. So, all of this is what many girls deal with in addition to any other anxiety that may come up. It stinks, and it is a lot of pressure.

Researchers have other theories that include our sex hormones—apparently not only are those cause for giggles from boys but they also might interact with our mood-regulating hormones. Women are also more likely to be survivors of physical or mental abuse, and this would make us more likely to have a trauma-related anxiety disorder (see the Harvard Medical School study mentioned earlier). Social expectations also pose possible reasons why women are more susceptible to anxiety.

Men might be just as anxious, but they have a tendency to self-medicate more than women do. Self-medicating is what the stereotypical male college student does—drinking and using drugs. It isn't as socially acceptable for women to do these things, so it is possible that fewer women try to overcome their fears with drinking or drugs. No matter what sex you are or how people stereotype you, drinking and drugging are horrendous and unproductive ways to deal with anxiety. It is a *very* bad idea! That means don't do them or get even an inkling of an idea in your head that they could be helpful to you.

Also, women are almost expected to have anxiety. It is somewhat acceptable for women to be shy, to project their need to be rescued by a knight in shining armor (you will become your own knight in shining armor, just you wait), and to demonstrate some dependence. Independent women are not really socially acceptable yet. What is wrong with this picture? Well, if we are sent messages that it isn't cool to be independent, but it is sweet and wonderful to be dependent, shy, and kind of weak—how do you think we will act? We probably won't act very strong. Luckily, this expectation is changing and you can help it change by becoming a strong and independent woman.

Take a moment to think about women who inspire you with their independence, strength, creativity, or actions. Hopefully you have someone close to you to look up to, but if you don't, admiring some of the cool women in recent history and the present is fine too. Beyoncé is pretty neat; she sings about being an independent woman and about being your own person. Hillary Clinton, although you may or may not appreciate her politics, is pretty tough as far as getting where she wants to be. Look back into history even more. There are women writers who changed literary history, took risks, and said to all of us women, "Hey, you are bigger than this. You are tough and strong and can get through anything. Don't let anxiety or self-consciousness hold you back."

Let's do some girl power activities to reinforce how much girls rule.

## Worry Word Search

```
A  B  C  I  M  I  O  P  R  L  S  T
L  M  O  R  N  N  S  T  R  O  N  G
P  O  W  E  R  D  I  P  M  U  Z  R
Y  U  M  L  P  E  E  L  R  I  G  O
T  O  U  G  H  P  O  Q  U  I  N  C
K  B  R  E  I  E  L  N  E  N  I  K
R  E  P  E  G  N  A  H  C  M  A  L
T  A  O  M  Q  D  Z  X  N  S  D  W
U  I  E  A  G  E  O  Z  P  M  R  E
H  B  L  F  P  N  F  R  S  T  L  N
U  O  D  S  Y  T  N  O  K  W  I  S
L  H  W  O  M  A  N  H  E  A  M  E
M  P  Y  T  E  I  X  N  A  Y  O  G
```

Find the following words:

| | | | |
|---|---|---|---|
| Strong | Girl | Tough | Independent |
| Change | Phobia | Power | Anxiety |
| Woman | Rock | | |

## Girl Power

What is it about being a teenage girl that makes you feel anxious? What about it makes you feel strong? For every anxiety you can name, find two strengths; they can be as insignificant as liking your pinky toe or as big as appreciating how strong you feel after running a mile. If you are having a hard time finding strengths within yourself, look at your friends or female role models and label their strengths.

**Sample**

## Anxiety:

*I freak out when I have to go to a party.*

## Strengths:

*I am really good at solitaire.*
*I am a really nice friend.*

**Your turn!**

## Anxiety:

## Strengths:

_____    _____

_____    _____

_____    _____

_____    _____

_____    _____

_____    _____

# Part II

■ ■ ■ ■ ■ ■ ■ ■ ■ ■

## Peer Pressure, Parents, School, Obsessions, Rituals—the List Goes On

In this section we will go over anxieties many teenage girls report—some with "clinical" names, and some without. Anxieties are quirky. One person might feel comfortable speaking in public but be anxious about flying; another might enjoy flying but dread public speaking.

# Chapter 4

## A Self-Made Pressure Cooker

Do you expect to be perfect—perfect grades, perfect friends, perfect at everything? Do you think others expect this of you? Your dad wants a perfectly clean room, your volleyball coach expects a perfect serve, your sister expects a perfect role model, your grandmother expects perfect manners, your friends expect you to react perfectly in every situation, your boyfriend expects you to be perfect in social situations, and your uncle expects perfect grades? Yikes! All of this pressure will keep you pretty tightly wound, and not much fun to be around!

We all have expectations for the people we care about or love. Usually expectations are meant to help us succeed and be our best, but often they can be overwhelming and make us feel like crap when we don't meet them. There is something important every teenager should know: You are never going to live up to *everyone's* expectations. No matter how hard you try, no matter how incredibly fabulous you are, you won't be able to do it. And it isn't because you stink that you can't do it; it is because people sometimes have unrealistic expectations of us, even if they care about us and love us. People who care about you, however, will often lighten up if they see you drowning under pressure. Some won't, and with those people, you might have to say to yourself, "I can try my hardest, but I probably won't quite meet their expectations and that is okay because I am proud of my efforts." It may sound totally cheesy, but cheese is what will get you through sometimes, so eat it up. You can't always control other people's expectations, but you can control your reactions to their expectations and recognize that you are a hard worker but that all the hard work in the world won't please everyone.

There is a set of expectations, however, that you do have complete control over. These are often very high and impossible to meet. They probably bother you more than any other expectations, and the person who put them on you is very close; if this person's expectations were achievable, you would probably feel a ton better. Who could it be? Who do you have to live with for the rest of your entire life—through high school, college, career, marriage, parenthood, retirement, and senior living? Mom? Siblings? Friends? Nope. You. You, you, you, you, you. There is nothing you can do to get away from yourself, so you'd better find a way to like yourself, not beat yourself up, and create healthy and achievable expectations. If you can do that, then you will be proud of yourself, successful in your own eyes, and content with your achievements. Other people's expectations won't seem that important if you can find peace through meeting your own expectations. Just make sure that they are expectations that are not overwhelming.

## ✎ Who's Creating the Pressure?

Pay attention to when you put pressure on yourself by noting what your expectations are of yourself. Is an A- on a test unacceptable? Do you stress out when you only study for one hour instead of two? If this is the case, you need to identify the unhealthy expectations and create some healthy ones!

In this exercise, you are going to write down your expectations of yourself in school, social situations, appearance, extracurricular activities (sports, yearbook, prom committee, etc.), family situations, and any miscellaneous situations where you might put expectations on yourself. After writing them down, you are going to look at them realistically to see if they are healthy or unhealthy. One easy way of determining whether they are unhealthy is to look at them as if they are expectations you have for your favorite person in the world; if you wouldn't expect something this high of someone you care about, should you expect it of yourself?

Once you have determined which expectations aren't so healthy, change them to something achievable that encourages solid effort on your part, but doesn't apply the pressure of perfection.

Here are a couple of examples:

*I expect to get straight As.* This is not very healthy. Would I expect my little sister to get straight As? No, but I would encourage her to try hard, so how can I reword this in a way that is kinder but still includes solid expectations?

*I expect to strive for As, and to try my hardest in my classes; if I try hard, I will probably get good grades, maybe even all As. If I don't get all As, that is okay because I put my best effort into my work.* Much better!

*I should be skinnier and lose weight. I will work out every day.* Again, this is not very healthy. Am I a healthy weight? Then why lose weight? I don't like or dislike people just because of what they weigh. If someone liked me because I was skinny, he or she probably wouldn't be a very good friend.

*I should try to maintain a healthy weight by working out and eating healthy foods. I will try to exercise a few times a week and eat more fruits and vegetables.* Now *that* sounds healthy.

Write down your expectations of yourself for key topics, determine whether they are healthy or unhealthy, and then rewrite the unhealthy ones:

School:

_____

_____

_____

_____

Social situations:

_____

_____

_____

_____

Appearance:

_____

_____

_____

_____

_____

Extracurricular activities:

_____

_____

_____

_____

Family situations:

_____

_____

_____

_____

Miscellaneous situations:

_____

_____

_____

_____

_____

## What's the Worst That Could Happen?

Do you ever expect the worst? When you are faced with anxiety, it is likely that you expect the worst from the situation you are about to encounter. For example, if you are heading to a party and very anxious, you might think, "I can't go. This is going to be awful. No one is going to talk to me. I'm going to look like a total loser."

Challenge this thinking. You were invited to the party, so someone probably does want to talk to you. Do you know people who are going? They will probably talk to you. If no one talks to you, what could you do? You could approach someone and strike up a conversation, pretend to text someone until someone approaches you, or sneak out if you are feeling truly overwhelmed. What about the loser part—do you think people who don't usually talk at parties are total losers? You probably don't even remember who talked to whom at recent parties you've attended.

If this worst-case scenario did come true, it probably wouldn't be the best night of your life, but it wouldn't be the worst either. You would live through it, your family would still love you, your house would still be standing, and so on. Sometimes thinking of the worst-case scenario can be helpful if you can pick it apart and use it to problem solve a little bit. You will also realize that even the worst-case scenario, although anxiety provoking, is manageable.

Pick five of your biggest anxieties and find solutions to the worst-case scenarios.

1. _____

_____

_____

_____

2. _____

_____

_____

_____

3. _____

_____

_____

_____

4. _____

_____

_____

_____

_____

5. _____

_____

_____

_____

# Chapter 5

## Food, Farts, and Fat

Your body is your body, whether it looks a certain way, makes noises, or is growling for food. Anxiety about bodily functions and how your body is changing can be very real and very stressful. They aren't really anxieties you can avoid, though, because we all need to eat, everyone farts (yes, *everyone*), and we all have fat on our bodies.

As far as food goes, eating is how we fuel our bodies. Just like gas for a car, we need something to keep us going. If food stresses you out, or eating in front of people makes you nervous, try to think of food as the necessity it is and not as a reason for people to judge you or for you to judge others. Boys tend to get away with this one more easily than girls. Boys have eating contests, many are trying to gain weight, and our society doesn't judge boys on how or what they eat. Being female comes with pressures about food. Not only are you supposed to have a minimal appetite, but also it seems as though girls and women judge each other on what, how much, and how neatly they eat. Eating needs to be about sustaining a healthy body and mind, as well as having fun with it every now and then by enjoying treats. It is also okay to be messy when you eat. Being comfortable eating in front of people will make them more comfortable eating in front of you, so you are helping out your friends by coming to peace with food, and eating when and what you want—messy or not!

Farts, burps, and blowing your nose: these are all relatively unavoidable noises that your body is going to make, and sometimes it will make them at the worst time in the world. You might fart during your first date with the boy of your dreams, burp during a presentation, or have to blow your nose during a test. All of these can happen, and it is likely that you will face a situation that is somewhat embarrassing. The burps and nose blowing are kind of easy to get over. Farts, on the other hand, are fabulous if you are a preteen boy who can fart long, loud, and stinky; but as a teenage girl, being a queen farter might not be a coveted title. Farts are just gases leaving our bodies. If you fart in public, you can either ignore it or make a joke out of it. But if you deny it and everyone knows you did it, jokes and ridicule will follow. The best way to deal with an embarrassing body moment is to laugh it off and pretend it didn't bother you at all. You can bury your face in a pillow if you must when you get home, but laughter is the best way to deflect any potential teasing.

Fat. Although people who live in the United States are heavier than ever, we seem to have an odd obsession with getting rid of fat and looking down at people who are fat. Girls are no longer alone with this social issue; boys are now dealing with it too. All girls have fat, and as they grow up it shows up on their body as curvy hips, big boobs, booties, and bellies. Fat can definitely make you self-conscious even if you have a normal, healthy amount. The distribution of fat clues everyone in to the fact that you are blossoming into a young woman. Fat finds your hips, boobs, and butt for a reason. It is actually preparing you for womanhood and childbearing. Try not to be ashamed of it. Instead, think of it as your body being amazing in preparing you for what could be if you decide kids are in your future. The body is really cool, so enjoy it and don't beat it up. It is the only one you have and you need to nourish it, let it make some noise, and do the work it is meant to do.

## My Most Embarrassing Moment

Write down your most embarrassing body moment *ever*. Did it destroy you? How did people react? Was it your defining moment? Let's pick apart that awful memory and make it one you can remember with a laugh. For example, say you farted at your senior week party in front of your boyfriend, two super-cool girls, and their two superhot boyfriends. As soon as you farted, the cutest of the boys pointed at you and said, "OMG, that was totally you!" As the color rushed to your face, you denied it. "It wasn't me! I think it was the chair hitting the wall funny." Everyone continues to laugh. For the rest of senior week, the boys in the group remind you of your fart.

Did this moment destroy you? No, but it was very embarrassing for the week. The lovely young woman who dealt it should have just admitted it was her and made a joke about it. Is this how anyone at that party remembers her? No, it is actually only the young woman who remembers it. The highlight of the week was the bonfire the next night. Is there humor here? Yes, it was funny and probably could have been made funnier if she had just made a joke about it. Then she could have been the girl who could laugh at a simple slip of gas.

Write down your most embarrassing moment. Does it still hang over your head? If so, would joking about it make it less of an issue about which people could poke fun? Was there anything funny about it for you? Is your life over because of it?

_____

_____

_____

_____

_____

_____

_____

## Body Love

You've only got one of them, so learning how to love it and accept it in spite of the anxiety it provokes is important. Label the parts of your physical self that make you the most anxious or uncomfortable and we will change those anxious thoughts into ones you can laugh at and learn to love. Look in the mirror and tell your most hated body part that you love it; give it a love pat and treasure it.

| Body Part: | What I hate about it: | Why it makes me strong/who I am: |
|---|---|---|
| *Big butt* | *Duh, it is huge!!* | *My aunt's is big like this too. It makes me strong; the butt is a really big muscle!! Plus, I can really shake my booty on the dance floor and skinny butts don't shake as well!* |
| _____ | _____ | _____ |
| _____ | _____ | _____ |
| _____ | _____ | _____ |
| _____ | _____ | _____ |
| _____ | _____ | _____ |
| _____ | _____ | _____ |

# Chapter 6

## Sex

The pressures to be sexually active and to dress provocatively are everywhere. Teens feel pressured by their peers, but they also feel pressured by media such as television shows, movies, magazines, and commercials. Sex seems to be everywhere, and ironically it is portrayed as the most fabulously romantic and wonderful act in which to partake. Sex can be great and fun and fantastic. It also can be fabulously romantic, but not when you do it before you are ready. When you have sex too young, there's no going back; you've done it. And unfortunately, once you've done it, whether it was horrible or fantastic, it is easier to do it again. It isn't such a big deal the second time, third time, fourth time . . . So you have to really think hard about your readiness to have sex. You may very well be sixteen, in love, and convinced that you are going to marry your significant other. If so, then there is no rush; you will be with your partner for the rest of your life, so wait until you are both really ready for sex and all the consequences that might follow. You may think sex is the way to keep your boyfriend or girlfriend interested. NO. It isn't. Once someone gets in your pants, the mystery is gone, and your self-respect might be too if you weren't ready. Treat your body with respect and expect the same of all of those you date or hang out with. It is rare that a teenage girl regrets waiting to have sex, but quite frequently a teenage girl regrets starting too soon. This is *your* body and you are in charge of keeping it healthy and happy. If *anyone* tries to force you to have sex, get away from the person, scream, or do whatever you need to do in order to protect yourself. This person is not deserving of your body and you have the right to protect it.

What are the potential consequences if you do have sex?

- **Pregnancy**—No matter what you decide to do about it, the decision will be with you forever. People think abortion or adoption is the easy way out, but both come with their own sets of emotions that you will feel throughout your life.
- **A baby**—A baby doesn't go away. The baby might be cute, and you might think a baby will love you forever, but a baby is a lot of work and a baby is with you whether you are in a good or bad mood, want to go to a party, have the flu, or whatever. A baby also yells, cries, and has temper tantrums.
- **Sexually transmitted diseases**—STDs are not at all pleasant and some can go unnoticed for years. Some have no cure, some can cause infertility, and some can make you itch, burn, grow warts, and have other painful consequences.
- **A broken heart**—Your heart may break as a teenager, young adult, or adult. If you are a teenager who has had sex for the first time and is dumped, however, that heartache will hurt a lot, especially if you regret having sex.
- **Loss of self-respect**—If you didn't want to have sex but had it anyway, you will have to live with that feeling of regret. It probably isn't going to bother your partner the way it bothers you.
- **Rumors**—Yeah, right; no one is going to find out! Even if you promise each other you will keep it a secret, chances are you will tell your best friend and your partner will tell his or her best friend. They might keep the secret for a while, but come on, things get around. Teens often tend to get mad at each other and spill secrets.
- **Insecurity**—Now that you've done the deed, what does your partner think of you? Were you good or bad? Did you know what you were doing? What if he or she dumps you? You might find that you are intensely clingy after the deed is done; that alone can scare someone away.
- **Disappointment**—The sex may have been awful, awkward, totally unpleasant, and embarrassing. This can throw a wrench in any relationship.

These are just a few of the consequences you might face. So how do you know if you are ready? Let's do some work to find out if you really are as ready as you think.

# ✎ Are You Ready?

Answer the following questions honestly and you will probably see some areas of uncertainty that will make you think twice about having sex.

1. Are you completely 100 percent in love with your partner and completely positive he or she feels the same way?
2. Are you afraid your partner will leave you if you don't have sex?
3. Is your partner pressuring you or making you feel guilty about not having sex?
4a. Have you gone over every potential scenario that could occur if you do have sex (pregnancy, STDs, insecurity, etc.)?
4b. Do you have the means to deal with such possible consequences? For example, do you and your partner have solid educations and full-time, lucrative jobs that would support a baby?
5. Are you emotionally prepared to deal with the possibility of getting dumped once you have sex?
6. Have you both gone to a teen clinic or doctor to get checked for any STDs? Even if you are both virgins, it is nice to have a clean bill of health.
7. Have you discussed contraception with each other and a safe adult such as a doctor or nurse?
8. Do you know how to put on a condom correctly? Go ahead and laugh, but you would be amazed at how few people (adults included) put them on correctly.
9. Are you even slightly nervous or afraid that you might not be ready?
10. Would your life be over if you didn't have sex with your partner?

Now take a look at your answers:

1. **YES.** That is awesome! You are in a loving relationship and can be intimate with each other in ways that don't involve sex. If your partner loves you 100 percent, then waiting will not bother your partner.
   **NO.** This is a no-brainer. No sex for you. Why would you want to have sex with someone you didn't think loved you unconditionally? Having sex with someone won't make that person love you

more; if someone suggests it will, that person is a total lame-o and doesn't deserve your body, mind, or heart.

2. **YES.** Your partner is lame and doesn't deserve you.
   **NO.** Good, there is no harm in waiting, and your partner doesn't sound like he or she is pressuring you.

3. **YES.** Peace out, home slice; get rid of this partner. Pressure or guilt is not cool.
   **NO.** Good, again. It sounds like your partner has great qualities and will handle waiting well.

4a. **YES.** Great! You and your partner have a very open relationship and are talking a lot, which is really important.
   **NO.** Start talking about these possibilities with your partner. This is a conversation you need to have if you are considering having sex. If you are too embarrassed or nervous to have this conversation, you aren't ready.

4b. **YES.** Really? Go over all of these things again. Most adults are barely ready for the consequences that come along with sex.
   **NO.** That is reason enough to wait.

5. **YES.** Then do you really want to have sex with this person? It doesn't sound like you like or trust your partner very much.
   **NO.** Then don't chance it.

6. **YES.** Awesome communication! This is a great move. Once you have a clean bill of health, though, why mess with it?
   **NO.** Do it! And if you find it too embarrassing, you aren't ready for the deed.

7. **YES.** Even more great communication! Fantastic!
   **NO.** Again, you have to do this. You must protect your body.

8. **YES.** Great! You must have paid attention during sex ed!
   **NO.** Learn how. It will help you for the rest of your life. It doesn't mean you have to try it out by having sex, but it is something you should know before you do have sex.

9. **YES.** Then wait.
   **NO.** Really? Not even a little bit?

10. **YES.** Then what's going on? Do you think you'll get dumped? That wouldn't be the end of your life; instead, it would be a new beginning with people who care about you!
   **NO.** Good, then don't hurry the love.

Okay, so that might have been a little bit one sided, but it was meant to get you thinking. Are you really ready for sex? Talk to a trusted adult, like a doctor, a nurse, or a counselor. Think about what having sex or waiting to have sex would mean for your relationship, and talk it over with your partner. Again, teens seldom regret waiting too long to have sex, but so many teens wish they had waited longer.

## How to Say "No" or "Not Yet"

It is hard to say no. When you are in the heat of the moment, feeling the love, your partner happens to have a condom, and you are home alone, it is really difficult to say, "Whoa! Wait a minute—let's think about this." Having a conversation about your readiness for sex prior to steaming up the windows will help. You will have already laid the groundwork, so the rest will just be reinforcement. Below are some suggestions on how to say no, followed by a space for you to come up with your own ideas. Once you figure things to say, you will practice saying them to a close friend or your mirror; seriously, if you hear yourself say them a few times, it will be much easier to express yourself in the moment. Let's plan for three different scenarios.

1. Prior to things getting steamy:
   "You are such a great kisser and everything, I can imagine what follows will be amazing. It is really important to me to wait until the right time when I can enjoy it without any regrets."

   Your turn: _____

   _____

   _____

   _____

   _____

   _____

2. Full steam ahead; things are hot and heavy:
   "OMG, I am not ready for this." [BREATHE] "Total buzz kill, but like we talked about, I need to wait until I am ready."

   Your turn: _____

   _____

   _____

   _____

   _____

   _____

3. We've gone past the steam...
   "No!! No, no, no. I enjoy this, but put your pants on, buddy. This is as far as it goes for now." (Now put *your* pants on and physically move away for a few minutes to let your hormones chill out.)

   Your turn: _____

   _____

   _____

   _____

   _____

   _____

Got those? Now say them in the mirror at least three times each!

# Chapter 7

## Drugs and Alcohol

The pressures to try mind-altering substances can start in elementary and middle school, and often get worse in high school and college. As a kid, you might know that you shouldn't try them because your parents said so, or you had a class in school that talked about saying no to drugs. As you get older, and you come across more people who smoke, drink, and experiment, it might not seem so bad. What's the big deal anyway? After all, Jenny smokes every day, but she does well in school and is class president; Jesse drinks every weekend, but he's still a star athlete and student; and Alanna has tried just about everything, but she's more fun than anyone else at parties. Plus, everyone's parents love her.

Seeing people use drugs and alcohol and still succeed socially, academically, athletically, and more, makes it hard to understand the dangers that underlie using these substances. For some people, experimenting a bit here and there might never result in any major catastrophe. But for others, one night of a drink too many, or the wrong combination of pills, could lead to life-changing events—including death. These people are not necessarily alcoholics or drug addicts; perhaps the first time they tried alcohol, they drank too much and a peer took advantage of them sexually, leading to a horrible spiral of depression and loss of self-respect. One time is all it takes—one night of drinking, one pill, one hit of marijuana laced with something. Just one time and your life can change forever.

So why does it seem so tempting? For the same reasons that it can be so dangerous. Not only are drugs and alcohol destructive to our bodies, they also lower inhibitions. People with anxiety may feel a lot better with fewer inhibitions. Of course, the lower your inhibitions, the more likely you are to make poor decisions, such as having unprotected sex, telling off a friend, taking a dare, driving drunk or with a drunk driver, trying a drug you never thought you would try, wandering off during a party, just to mention a few. Drugs and alcohol may be very dangerous for people with anxiety; they take the edge off and lead to people feeling like they must have a drink before they go to a party because they'll feel more relaxed. And this doesn't just happen with teenagers.

Adults often engage in this type of behavior too, and they may have unintentionally taught you that this is normal. If you hear your father say he "needs" a couple of beers to loosen up before he deals with his in-laws, or your aunt comment that a glass of wine is what she needs to gear up and go socialize, you are hearing how adults use alcohol to deal with anxieties or stressors. It doesn't mean these people are alcoholics, but it sends a message that using alcohol to deal with the world is acceptable when, in fact, it isn't—especially for an underage member of society like you.

If you can learn skills now to help you feel less anxious in a variety of settings, you won't need drugs or alcohol to help you get through a meeting, party, date, or other event. In the chapters to come, you will learn about these coping skills and maybe you can become an example to the adults around you who use drugs or alcohol. It is much safer to do a brief meditation before walking into a party than it is to slam down a few shots. Plus, with healthy coping skills, you stay yourself—not an altered version of yourself, but *you*. You have control over what you say and do. You can leave the situation knowing you didn't do something just because you were drunk or high that you'll later regret. No one can promise you won't make poor decisions sober, because we all do. But at least you'll be able to handle the decision as simply a poor decision, not a drunken disaster.

## What's Inside?

Do you really know what you are putting in your body? Find out! (*Circle the letter that represents your best guess.*)

1. A joint has _____ ounces of marijuana.

   **A**  10
   **B**  1
   **C**  Half an ounce
   **D**  You never know

2. A mixed drink has _____ ounces of alcohol.

    **A**  6
    **B**  4
    **C**  Depends on who makes it
    **D**  12

3. The amount of alcohol in an average 12-ounce bottle of beer is equal to the amount of alcohol in:

    **A**  One 5-ounce glass of wine
    **B**  One 1.5-ounce shot
    **C**  Neither one; beer has the most
    **D**  Both

4. What can you do to sober up faster?

    **A**  Eat peanut butter
    **B**  Nothing; time is the only way
    **C**  Drink a lot of coffee
    **D**  Eat a greasy meal

5. Marijuana can be laced with:

    **A**  Cocaine
    **B**  PCP
    **C**  Heroin
    **D**  All of the above

6. OxyContin is most similar to:

    **A**  Xanax
    **B**  Cocaine
    **C**  Heroin
    **D**  Alcohol

7. Taking someone else's prescription drugs isn't as bad as taking a street drug because:

    **A**  Someone you trust gave it to you.
    **B**  Any drug is bad unless you are being monitored by a doctor who has prescribed it specifically for you.
    **C**  The pharmacy wouldn't give out something that could kill you.
    **D**  Your friend's mom takes it all the time and she seems fine.

8. How do you know if someone is sober enough to drive?

   **A**  She said she has driven drunker than she is now and was fine.

   **B**  You can never tell. Pick someone who isn't drinking.

   **C**  It has been an hour since his last drink.

   **D**  She seems totally fine; she isn't slurring her words or walking funny.

## Answer Key

1. **D**. You never know! It depends on who rolled it, what it is cut with, where it came from, and other things. Even if you know the "dealer," you still never know what else might be in there.

2. **C**. Although many mixed drinks have a specific recipe, you can never tell who might be heavy handed with the alcohol.

3. **D**. Both. A 12-ounce beer = a 5-ounce glass of wine = a 1.5-ounce shot.

4. **B**. Time is the only way. Nothing is going to make you sober up faster.

5. **D**. All of the above. And the scary thing is, you never know what could be in there. Even if you really trust the people you are with, the person who had it before them could have put something in it and you wouldn't even know.

6. **C**. Heroin. Unfortunately, many people think OxyContin is less dangerous since it is a prescription drug, but any addictive drug is dangerous.

7. **B**. Any drug that is not prescribed for you is dangerous to take. Just because a drug comes in a bottle, that doesn't make it "safer" or "okay" to try without a doctor's monitoring.

8. **B**. You never know. Some people will claim to be great drunk drivers, or that they are fine and not drunk, but alcohol causes impairment as soon as you have one drink!

 **Off the Sauce**

Turning down drugs and alcohol is not always as easy as "just saying no." Sometimes there are peer pressures that can make saying a simple "no" overwhelming. As time goes on and you feel more confident in your decision to stay away from drugs and alcohol, saying a firm "No" or "No, thank you" will be simple. Also, people will respect your decision and stop asking or expecting you to have a drink or drug. Until then, there are some ways of saying "no" that won't put you on the spot. We've given some examples. As you did in the last chapter, think up some of your own ways to say "no" and practice, practice, practice!

1. The humor approach:
   "None for me, thanks. My mom breathalyzes me when I get home!"

   Your turn: _____

   _____

2. Change the topic:
   "Oh, thanks, but I'm all set for now. Hey, I saw you talking to Jenna yesterday. Are you two an item?"

   Your turn: _____

   _____

3. Something is coming up:
   "Not tonight. I have a big track meet tomorrow."

   Your turn: _____

   _____

As you start to feel more confident, the simplest answer will hopefully be "No, thank you. I don't drink or do drugs."

# Chapter 8

## POS (Parent over Shoulder)

Parents, guardians, and caregivers: they will be over your shoulder for all of your teenage years. Learning how to deal with the stress of others controlling your life is tough but manageable. As a teenager, it is natural to feel like spending less time with your parents, gaining more freedom, and keeping certain aspects of your life private. Unfortunately, as you start to feel this way, your parents or caregivers are probably feeling exactly the opposite. As you try to spend more time doing your own thing, they want to keep you closer. Giving you more freedom means trusting you, your friends, and people they might not even know; they will have to trust your judgment about people you meet, drinking, drugs, and more (FYI—this is a *very* scary step for an adult!). As you try to keep your life private—and you need and deserve privacy—the adults in your life may feel as though you are hiding something from them. In their fearful adult minds, this means, "WARNING: She is up to no good; she is at that age where sex, drugs, and danger are everywhere. If she is looking for privacy, she must be doing something naughty."

Now, the adults might be right; maybe you *are* up to no good. If so, keep in mind that if you get caught, gaining freedom or privacy in the future is going to stink because you have now given your parents reason not to trust you and to deny you more freedom. If you simply want privacy for privacy reasons and more freedom for independence reasons, you deserve it! Getting the adults in your life to go along with this can be rather tricky. But remember, as annoying as they may be and as in your business as they try to get, they were teenagers once too. This means two very important things for you. First, they were once desperate for privacy just like you. (You will probably have to help them remember this since they are getting into old fart age.) Second, they have life experience, which means there is a reason why your growing up frightens them. Maybe they had a bad drinking experience, sex too soon, or a friend who was hurt in a drunk driving accident. Everyone goes through something during those teenage years. The adults in your life are trying to protect you from the negative experiences they encountered. While this is a noble goal, it isn't realistic. You are going to have pain, face danger, make mistakes, and potentially have regrets. Working *with* the adults in your life (instead of screaming at them and telling them you hate them and they are *sooo* unfair even if that is how you feel) will help you avoid some of the dangers of adolescence while you gain some extra freedom and privacy.

 ## Pick Apart Your Parents

What is it that your parents do that drives you the craziest? Is there a reason they might be doing that which might be for your benefit?

This is an easy one. You probably pick apart the adults in your life already, so now you are just going to write these gripes down. Think about what you say to your friends about your parents or guardians. For example, do you *hate* that your mother makes you check in by phone every hour? Does your father check your schoolbag on a daily basis?

Now think about why they might do these things other than to ruin your social life and snoop on you. Did you forget to inform your mom that you were changing hangout spots one night and, when she needed you in an emergency, she didn't know where to find you? Did your dad have a friend or brother who used to stash his cigarettes in his schoolbag, so now he checks yours all the time?

If you can't think of a valid reason why they have set certain limits or laid down certain rules, ask them!

HINT: When you ask, do so at the right time, like not while they are angry with you, not on their way out the door, and not when you are on punishment. Ask while you are all home for the afternoon and relaxing. Don't accuse them of being too harsh; instead, own up to mistakes you may have made that caused them to make the rules they've set for you. For example: "Hey, I was wondering, how come you want me to check in every hour? Is it because of that time I...."

Or put a little humor in there followed by a serious question: "Dad, do you find my backpack that interesting? Are you worried that I'll hide something from you?"

The approach is key! If you demonstrate an open mind, the adults will be more likely to answer with an open mind, and maybe even reconsider some of their rules.

What drives me bonkers about the adults in my life:

_____

_____

_____

_____

Why might they do or expect these crazy things? (Try not to write things like, "Because they hate me . . . because they are bananas," or other such reasons!)

_____

_____

_____

_____

Are any of these reasons valid? If not, talk to them. If the reasons are valid, but still seem suffocating, talk to them. Talking to your parents is probably not a priority right now, but it could really help you gain their trust and therefore more freedom and control over your privacy.

## Chatting with the "Enemy"

Here are some strategies on how to talk to your parents about reconsidering limits and rules without totally offending them:

1. Adults are *not* the enemy. Stop thinking of them this way and instead try thinking, "This is an adult who cares about me, worries about my well-being, and is trying to keep me safe."

2. Put the ball in their court: "Mom, I was hoping we could talk about some things that are on my mind. Is now a good time?" If it isn't, don't give up. Schedule some time with her. Maybe she'll want to have the conversation over ice cream when younger siblings are in bed, or when your grandmother is out of earshot.

3. Create a list (in your head or on paper) of what you want changed, what you have done to earn a change in rules, and some things that you are willing to do to earn a change. For example, if your curfew is ten o'clock on weekends and everyone else has a curfew of eleven o'clock, DON'T say you deserve a later curfew because everyone else has one. Instead, say, "I was wondering if we could talk about changing my curfew. I have never been late for my curfew and many of the social events I go to don't wind down until eleven. Is there a way I can earn a later curfew?" This points out that you have been responsible for your curfew thus far, that you are willing to do something to earn the later curfew, and that you are still putting the control of the curfew in the adults' hands.

4. Own up to any mistakes you have made in the past. Do your parents drive you everywhere because you lied to them about where you and your friends were going one night? If so, show that you have learned from that error: "I know I really screwed up when I violated your trust and lied to you about where Sarah and I were going. Is there any way to prove to you that I have learned from that mistake and won't do it again?" Pause for any answer they may have. Then say something like:

    "I had an idea. I was thinking maybe we could start out small and I could drive places with my friends during the day, but you could still drive me at night. Once you feel like I'm doing the right thing, we could try some nighttime rides with friends and I could call you from wherever we go so you know that I'm really there." Honesty works. Making excuses or lying will always get you in the end; even if no one catches you, you still know that you violated their trust.

5. Listen to what these adults are saying. If they insist on looking through your entire room on a daily basis, find out why and listen to their reasoning. It might be completely irrational, but listening to their reasoning will help you point out *kindly and respectfully* that this is excessive. For example, your dad might say, "I know what I did when I was your age and I don't want you making those mistakes. I didn't tell my parents anything. I hid all my drugs in my room and I don't want you screwing up like I did." You can say, "I know you are really worried about that, Dad, and I love that you care about me so much, but I am fifteen years old and I need some privacy. I have learned from you that drugs are bad and I am not doing them, so is there any way we could cut down on the frequency of these room checks or if I could have a lockbox for some personal items that are hands-off to you? Is there anything I've done to make you think I've doing drugs?"

   Reiterate to the adult that you heard him or her, that you appreciate the concern, you are willing to offer some peek into your life, and you are willing to answer questions.

6. Be respectful. You are not going to get anywhere with your folks if you yell at them, tell them they are stupid, stomp off, express the unfairness of it all by slamming doors. None of that is going to work.

7. DON'T FLIP OUT if they say no. Take a deep breath. Express that you understand, but that you would like to revisit the situation in the future since it is something about which you feel strongly. Continue to follow the rules the way they are and find a time a month or so away to bring it up again.

8. Start small. Tackle a small rule first. Once you have your communication with your caring adults down, and have proved to them that changing some rules was a good idea because you handled things responsibly, then you can tackle the bigger rules.

9. Consider family therapy. If the rules are truly irrational and the adults in your life will not listen to you at all, you might consider bringing up going to family therapy. You could tell the adults that you don't feel as though you are communicating with them

effectively and would like to learn how you could all better communicate with one another.

10. Involve adults in your daily life. Let the adults in your life share in your life and they may start to feel more a part of it and less like dictators. Instead of answering "Fine" when you are asked how your day was, tell them about something that happened during your day. If you are going out, tell them who you are going with and where you will be. Opening up to caring adults will help them recognize that you do want to involve them in your life—just not all the time!

# Chapter 9

## How Do I Look?

Obsessing over how you look can literally take over your whole life. It can also become detrimental to your health, if it takes the form of eating disorders or body dysmorphic disorder. We live in a culture that is obsessed with how people look. Movie stars discover pictures of their cellulite plastered over the tabloids, magazines speculate that actresses are pregnant when their stomachs are flat instead of concave, and diet commercials are everywhere. Avoiding feeling pressure to look perfect can be nearly impossible, especially for a teenage girl. If you do not worry about how you look, that is awesome. *Awesome*. Really.

It is so hard for some people not to worry, so if you are someone who doesn't worry, please help your girlfriends see that looks really aren't the most important part of life. No one will remember how your hair was cut in seventh grade; people will remember you for who you were and how you influenced their lives. Maybe you helped someone study for a test; maybe you were really nice to a new kid. These things have nothing to do with how you look. How you look doesn't dictate how talented you are, how smart you are, how nice you are, how hard you study, or what a reliable friend you are. Looks have nothing to do with these traits, which really reveal who you are. Everyone is beautiful when she acts kind or helps others; it is often that great inner beauty that outshines the girl with the nicest smile, best clothes, glossiest hair, and kickin' body.

HINT: If you find that you beat yourself up about how you look, challenge yourself to find something every day that you like about how you look—even if the thing you like about yourself is nothing more significant than a freckle on your toe. If so, love that freckle and that toe!

So what the heck is body dysmorphic disorder? Someone with body dysmorphia has become fixated on a part of her (or his) body, so much so that it interferes with how she lives her life. For example, maybe your ears stick out, so you have decided never to play a sport where you have to wear your hair back, or you won't cut your hair short because then it couldn't hang over your ears. Maybe you won't even swim because your hair will be slicked back and your ears will be more noticeable. This is a disorder that can really get in the way of you being you. If you are so self-conscious about something that you basically plan your life around it, you aren't living life to the fullest. If body dysmorphia is a problem for you, talk to the adults in your life about seeking help from a counselor. It may be just what you need.

## Mirror, Mirror

Take this quiz to find out if your obsession with your appearance has gone too far.

1. When you get ready in the morning, you:

    A   Already know what you are wearing; you plan for the week, not just for the next day!

    B   Have a general idea of what you will wear; you hate to be rushed in the morning.

    C   Have no clue; hopefully, there is something clean on your floor.

2. If you have a zit that is in a really noticeable place, you:

    A   Consider not going to school or don't go; zits are like an illness!

    B   Cover it up as best as possible and move on; it will go away eventually.

    C   Groan with annoyance—*if* you even notice it.

3. When people want to take pictures of you, you:

    A   Freak out; you are so ugly, you don't want it frozen in time.

    B   Try to remember the poses that they recommend in magazines to make you look your best.

    C   Smile, or make a crazy face. Fun!

4. Someone makes a comment that you don't look good today. You:

   **A** Run to the bathroom, obsess over what looks "wrong," and let the comment ruin the rest of your day.

   **B** Internally sneer at the person, check yourself out in the mirror, and accept that today might not be your best day, but she is no beauty queen either.

   **C** Reply, "No kidding! I didn't sleep last night and I don't have hours to spend on my makeup like you do."

5. Your pants feel tight. You

   **A** Worry for the rest of the day that you are fat and everyone thinks you are a moose, decide you will not eat any more junk, and spend all your extra time at the gym.

   **B** Hope it is because you just took them out of the dryer, and think about whether you should change your afternoon candy bar to a piece of fruit some days.

   **C** Change into comfy pants. Who wants to feel uncomfortable?

## Answer Key

If you answered mostly:

**As:** EEEK! One zit makes you freak! Sounds like you spend an awful lot of time freaking out about your appearance. That precious time could probably be used for something much more important and fun.

**Bs:** Cool. You have a healthy concern with how you look, but it doesn't get in the way of your daily activities.

**Cs:** Good for you. Looks aren't really a priority at all; share that self-esteem with others!

## Inside Out

Find the beauty within yourself and let it outshine the beauty you have on the outside. There are a few different ways to do this activity—supercrafty, pseudocrafty, or simple crafty.

1. To get started, collect copies of pictures and words that represent inner beauty, strength, and dreams to you—maybe a picture of your grandmother, a female actor you find really talented, a funny picture of you and your best friend, your favorite summer vacation spot, a poem you have written, a picture of sneakers because you love to run, a picture of a stethoscope because you want to go to med school. Put them in an envelope and set it aside.

2. Now, collect copies of pictures and words that represent how you think others will see you or what they associate with you. These can be connected to the images from step 1, or be completely different. Maybe you're known for your awesome skills at doing eye makeup, or for your superlong hair. Maybe you're the class clown. Cut out pictures of a big red nose or crazy shoes. Put them in another envelope and set it aside.

3. Think about how you want to be viewed by others. Do you want others to remember you as class clown or would you prefer they remember you for your poetry? Now dump out both envelopes and split everything into two piles with that in mind: One—how you want people to remember you, and what you find most important and special about yourself. Two—how people view you now, parts about your life that aren't the most important to you, but are still parts of you. Take any remaining cutouts and toss them. If you don't want to be remembered for those things or see them as unimportant, get rid of them!

4. Okay, here is where you pick how crafty you want to be:

   **Simple Crafty**—Get a notebook (or poster board) and glue your pictures and words to the pages. This is meant for your use only, so if you use a poster board but don't want anyone's eyes but your own looking at it, be sure you can hang it somewhere discreet like your closet. Using a notebook can be helpful because you can stash it more easily.

   **Pseudocrafty**—Using a poster board, glue the pile of the most meaningful pictures and words in the middle. This represents your core: who you are, and who you want to be. Surrounding your core, glue the pictures and words that aren't the most important, but are still a part of your being.

   **Supercrafty**—Get a shoebox or an inexpensive wooden box at a craft store. Make sure you have glue that will work on that surface. Glue the most important pictures and words to the *outside* of the box. This may be how you feel on the inside, but let it out! Put it on the outside. For the items that aren't as important to you, glue those to the inside. They are still a part of you—just not the most important part.

5. This is for you, and not for anyone else. If you want to share it, great, but if you are too nervous to show people that you are interested in being a doctor or a poet, or that you don't really care about having the best clothes, don't share it. Keep it to yourself and look to it as inspiration on how you want to be and who you want to be. Don't lose sight of your bigger goals in the chaos of trying to look fabulous. It isn't worth it. You are so much more than the superficial stuff that seems important right now. You are a poet, a granddaughter, a friend, an animal lover, a runner. You are not your butt—big or skinny. You are not your hair or the zit on your nose. You are you, and no matter how bad a hair day you might be having, nothing can take away what is on the inside and who you really are.

# Chapter 10

## I Can't Go to That Party...

Social anxiety can be sneaky, and it may not seem particularly harmful at first. It can start by canceling plans at the last minute and then suddenly turn into never going out with your friends. Social anxiety can change depending on the situation, your mood, and the closer the event gets. You may be perfectly comfortable going to a huge concert with your best friend, but the thought of going to a small party with everyone from high school—including your best friend—may make getting a head start on your homework sound like a great alternative. If you had a great week at school and everything is going well, you might have no problem going to the football game with your friends, but if the past week has been stinky and your mood is lowered, that football game might cause you to hyperventilate and cancel your plans. You may be psyched by your friend's party on Saturday, talk to her about it, pick out your outfit, take a shower, do your hair, and head toward the door. But, as you start to leave, you might be gripped suddenly by fear, and then call your friend with some crazy excuse.

Social anxiety can come and go. It might be mild on some days and feel like stage fright on others. It can really make your social life a disaster. The more you blow off parties and activities, the easier it becomes to avoid them and the harder it will be to go to social events. Eventually, people may stop inviting you to them. When you confront them about it, they might point out that you cancel at the last minute, don't want to go places anyway, or leave early once you go out. So where does social anxiety come from, and what can you do about it?

Social anxiety seems to be related to self-esteem. If you are self-conscious, going to a party can feel overwhelming. What do you say when you get there?

What if no one talks to you? What if the girl who is often mean to you is there and she makes a snide comment about your outfit? Just the thought that someone might find fault in us—what we talk about, how we look, or how we act—can make us feel like we are on stage being judged.

Teenage life does involve a great deal of judgment by others, whether you like it or not. But if you keep in mind that the only person's opinion that really matters is yours, you might be able to push your anxiety aside and have fun. If you are worried about what people might think, imagine who else might be worried—namely, almost everyone. Instead of remembering that you didn't have anything cool to talk about at a party, your peers might be worrying that they had nothing cool to talk about! The good thing and bad thing about being a teenager is that teens tend to be self-focused. So while your own mistakes may seem horrific to you, they are often forgotten by your peers—who are thinking about their own mistakes or social follies.

## ✎ Get Back in the Game

Setting goals for getting out and becoming more sociable is a bit like setting exercise goals. One type of goal you might set is to plan to go to an event for a short amount of time. If you are having fun, you can stay longer, but you *must* stay for the planned amount of time. For example, if your friend is having a party, tell her you can come for a little bit and plan to stay for twenty minutes. Set an alarm on your cell phone so that you don't spend the twenty minutes staring at a clock, but instead are mentally present at the party. When your alarm goes off, you can make an escape or stay a little longer. As you commit to social events and stay for an allotted amount of time, you can increase the amount of time you stay until you are comfortable going out!

Another type of goal you can set is to plan one thing you wish to accomplish at an event. For example, if your fear of parties is that no one will talk to you, go to a party with the goal of saying "hello" to one person. The worst that can happen is that the person you want to talk to will blow you off. If so, that person is totally not worth your time anyway. Start out with someone you feel comfortable with and move on to people you don't know very well. You might even meet new friends this way!

A third type of goal you might set is to agree to go to an event if you can count on having some support. Talk to a good friend about your fears and ask her to promise to stay with you for the first thirty minutes of a party. This can do a lot to reduce your anxiety. She can be the person you will talk to, or she can serve as a buffer in case others come up to chat. Make sure she is trustworthy and will honor her promise. Someone who leaves you hanging is not going to be very helpful. As time goes on, she can agree to spend the first twenty minutes with you and then check in on you after a ten-minute break. Baby steps and supportive friends can really help.

Once you have accomplished some goals, such as going to a party for twenty minutes, saying "hello" to a girl in your computer class, or standing at a get-together for five minutes by yourself, give yourself a ton of credit! Try all of these strategies, mixed with each other or on their own, and write down what your biggest fears were while trying them. How were you able to manage? Did you get through twenty minutes by singing a song over and over again in your head? Did you say "hello" to someone new by practicing what you would say before you said it? Figure out how you did it; this will help you in any social situation!

Goal: _____

_____

_____

What was scary? _____

_____

_____

What helped? _____

_____

_____

What felt good about accomplishing it? _____

_____

What is my goal for next time? _____

_____

 ## What Social Situations Make Me Freak?

Some people love to speak in front of large crowds, yet the thought of going to an intimate dinner makes them sweat. What gets to you?

1. Family events make me want to fake an illness (out of anxiety, not boredom!)

   **YES │ NO**

2. Speaking in front of a crowd of people I don't know sounds like torture.

   **YES │ NO**

3. Speaking in front of people I know makes me anxious.

   **YES │ NO**

4. Large crowds make me nervous.

   **YES │ NO**

5. Small parties or events make me self-conscious.

   **YES │ NO**

6. Going up to get an award or have something presented to me is a nightmare.

   **YES │ NO**

7. Walking into a party or event alone is so hard that it's not worth going.

   **YES │ NO**

Where do you experience anxiety? Is it with family? Is it with people you don't know? Do you experience it at small gatherings? All of the above scenarios? Set goals based on your answers. Challenge yourself to be more comfortable with situations in which you feel the least comfortable.

# Chapter 11

## Cat Got Your Tongue?

Does the thought of speaking in public make you pray the earth will swallow you? For some, this fear goes hand in hand with social anxiety; for others, it can really affect school performance. Most people have their first experience with public speaking in school. School is where you are called on (hand raised or not), where oral presentations are expected, and where you need to showcase and defend your knowledge. Your anxiety about speaking in public may be due to fear of sounding like an idiot, not wanting to be the center of attention, being unsure of the subject matter, or just an overall feeling of self-consciousness. Whatever the reason, practice really does decrease anxiety. The more public speaking you do, the more confident you will become in many areas.

Working with your teachers is a great way to help break down this anxiety. Most teachers are happy to help since they know it will increase your performance in their class, as well as help you be successful in other classes and in your future. Not raising your hand enough or contributing to class discussion can often make you seem disinterested, as if you haven't done the work, and can even lower your grade. If you can get comfortable speaking in class, you can get comfortable speaking just about anywhere!

### Pick Me! Pick Me!

If getting called on in class is where your fear finds its stronghold, this is the activity for you. Find a teacher with whom you are comfortable or a guidance counselor who will help you talk to a teacher about this project.

Explain to the teacher that you would like to work on being more comfortable answering questions in class and believe that he or she can help you make the fear of raising your hand disappear.

**Phase 1:** Come up with a question for your teacher to ask during class. Present your teacher with the answer prior to class and have your teacher help you make the answer sound just right. In class, your teacher will ask the question and call on you—whether or not your hand is up. You already know the answer, so this will be a no-brainer.

Try this two or three times in one week and move on to Phase 2.

**Phase 2:** Have your teacher give you a question the night before class. Go home and research the question. Prior to class, show your teacher your prepared answer and make sure it sounds great. In class, answer when called on!

Try this two times in one week and move on to Phase 3.

**Phase 3:** Have your teacher give you a general idea of a question that will be asked in class—maybe the paragraph it will come from, or the worksheet where you can find the answer. Study that section extra hard (of course study the rest too!) and be ready for questions the next day. Prior to class, have your teacher ask a couple of different questions about the topic and see how you do. During class, get ready to raise your hand when the subject matter comes up; otherwise, be ready to be called on—your teacher knows you know the answer!

**Phase 4:** Look back on your success and smile! You have answered questions in class and answered them correctly! If you start to feel anxious, go back a phase and work with your teacher on building your confidence.

Get ready to see that class participation grade soar like your hand!

## A First-Class Class Presentation

You may find that you look forward to doing presentations once you have a few good ones under your belt. Here are some tips on presenting with class.

1. Note cards or paper? Do you work better with note cards to glance at or notes on paper? Pick one and stick to it. Whatever you pick, be sure to number each paper or card in case you drop your notes on your way up to present.
2. Make eye contact, breathe, smile. Write hints on your notes. On every third note card, draw a set of eyes to remind you to make eye contact with someone or to at least lift your head up for a moment. After every major point, draw something that reminds you to breathe and count to three so that you aren't just plowing

through your notes. Find spots to draw a smile. You can smile to yourself or smile to your class; just make sure you smile a couple of times during your presentation—even if you have to force it.

3. Practice, practice, practice. Practice alone, but do the presentation out loud and use a mirror. Make eye contact with yourself and give yourself a smile; you can do this. When you are ready, practice in front of someone who will be honest and give you constructive feedback. Consider asking your teacher and a classmate if you can use them to look at when you make eye contact; their encouraging looks or smiles will help you relax.

4. Visualize. The night before your presentation, practice once more, then close your eyes and visualize how well your presentation will go the next day. Imagine you are calm, your friends are ready to make eye contact when you need it, and you have rehearsed enough to almost know your presentation by heart. Visualize a great outcome and positive results may follow.

5. Present! You can do this. You have done it on your own, in front of others, and you have visualized it going well. Now get up there and do it!

6. Feedback. Ask your teacher for feedback and advice about your presentation. If your teacher points out major flaws, ask if you can try it again in front of him or her after getting a chance to correct anything that may have gone awry. Teachers love being experts. If you ask them for help and then use their feedback, they usually will be very appreciative!

   Give yourself feedback: Is there anything you wish had gone differently? If so, what? How can you change it the next time? Make notes about what you would do differently and keep them with your teacher's feedback. The next time you do an oral report, look back at this information and try to improve!

## Once upon a Time...

Volunteer in your community. You might be surprised at how many opportunities there are to volunteer to read aloud to people at a library, day-care center, elementary school, or school for the blind. Volunteering to read aloud will give you great practice in public speaking as well as make you feel good about helping your community.

# Chapter 12

## Did I Unplug My Curling Iron?

Do you worry about things so much that they take up your whole day? Do you have to go through certain rituals just to get out of the house? These sound like obsessive-compulsive behaviors and they can really put a kink in your life. Have you ever watched a baseball game and noticed when some players are up at bat they have to tap their bat four times, tighten their gloves, and then shake their butts? Maybe you have a friend who plays a sport and she refuses to use anything but her lucky ponytail holder on game day?

Do you have any habits that are similar to these? Rituals here and there are fine—as long as you don't freak out or lose your cool if you aren't able to complete the ritual. For example, say you eat three pieces of toast every time you have a science test, and when you get up in the morning, you find that there are only two pieces of bread left. Instead of thinking, "Bummer, I really like to have three, but two will have to do," you think, "Oh no! My day is ruined! My family is so selfish! They wolfed down most of the bread and only left two slices for me! Now I am going to fail my test!" If you focus on how you will now fail the test because you only had two pieces of toast instead of on how well you prepared for the test, your thinking needs a little tweaking.

Another example of an obsessive behavior is worrying about shutting off appliances or locking windows and doors. Unfortunately what starts off as healthy double-checking may become triple- and quadruple-checking, which can make you late for all your plans! Some people feel a need to turn the appliance off and turn it on again and off again to make sure it really is off. This can become time-consuming and stressful. These rituals might help ease fears about shutting things off or locking them, but usually people who are prone to this type of worry will still worry once they leave the house. "Did I really unplug my curling iron? I locked the bathroom window, right? Maybe I should go back and check!" This type of worrying can eat up your day and put a serious crimp in your social life. If your friends are meeting for dinner at seven and you show up at seven-thirty, you missed valuable time with them. If you worry about whether you shut the oven off while your friends catch up on the latest "who dumped whom" news, you could miss some serious dish. So let's look at a few ways you can help calm this worrying so you can stop it before it takes away from socializing.

## Don't Worry!

Well, not *all* the time. Set aside "worry time" or "ritual time" and stop yourself when the time is up. It might take a ton of practice, but by doing this, you actually can cut down on the time you spend obsessing and worrying. If you are going out with your friends, set an alarm on your cell phone or iPod for two hours into the night. When this alarm goes off, you are allowed to worry. Not until then! If you catch yourself worrying before then, say to yourself, "Okay, I'm worried about this, but I'm having fun 'friend time,' and I have a time set aside for when I can worry. Hang in there and focus on what Jenny is saying—I think she just said Matt and Erica broke up again!"

If rituals are your vice, plan time to fit your ritual in before you leave the house. If you need to leave by four, plan to be ready by ten minutes to four and allow yourself ten minutes to go through your ritual. Once ten minutes is up, make yourself leave the house—no matter what! Social life, school life, and life in general await. If you waste time on these rituals, you will miss out on so much. As you get better at keeping your ritual to ten minutes, challenge yourself to carry it out in nine minutes. Keep decreasing the time spent on these rituals little by little and maximize studying and socializing time.

Put technology to use. Do you have a camera phone or some sort of device that takes pictures? Is the thought of your curling iron burning down the house bothering you all day in school? Then use one of these devices to take a picture of your unplugged curling iron before you leave the house. If you are stressed before that science test that your house has gone up in flames, check out your picture. The curling iron is unplugged!

Every time you use one of these coping skills successfully, kudos to you! If these skills don't work for you even after trying them time and time again, talk to an adult in your life about getting some help from a counselor or doctor.

 **Am I a Worry Wart?**

Does worrying about rituals take up valuable time in your day?

Keep track of how much time you spend worrying or practicing certain rituals. Include how it affected any plans. Did it make you late? Did it make you rush? Did it distract you from a test or conversation with friends?

**Example:**

| Worrying/Ritual | Time Spent | How It Affected My Day |
|---|---|---|
| *Shutting curling iron on and off* | *7–7:15 a.m. (15 minutes)* | *Late for school* |
| *Is my curling iron off?* | *7:15–9 a.m. (1 hour 45 minutes)* | *Distracted in English class and homeroom* |
| *Had to go home and check* | *2–2:20 p.m. (20 minutes)* | *Rushed home from school to check curling iron and missed out on hanging out with friends* |

Total time spent worrying: . . . . . . . . *2 hours 20 minutes*

What could I do with that time? . . . . *See a movie, study, hang with friends, veg out*

Does it affect my life? . . . . . . . . . . . *YES! YES! YES!*

**Your turn!**

Be honest. This activity is for your eyes only and is meant to help you, not horrify you. This is a behavior you can change with practice! Plus, the rewards of changing it are huge; think of all the time you will earn back!

| Worrying/Ritual | Time Spent | How It Affected My Day |
|---|---|---|
|  |  |  |
|  |  |  |
|  |  |  |

| Worrying/Ritual | Time Spent | How It Affected My Day |
|---|---|---|
|  |  |  |
|  |  |  |
|  |  |  |

Total time spent worrying: _____

_____

_____

What could I do with that time? _____

_____

_____

_____

Does it affect my life? _____

_____

_____

_____

# Chapter 13

## I Stink at Everything!

Like trying to be perfect, believing you stink at everything is a type of black-and-white thinking. There is always gray or middle ground; you just have to find it. Have you ever met anyone who actually stinks at everything? Even if you think your sibling stinks in general and thus stinks at everything, you can probably find one thing she does well. In fact, she might be really great at driving you crazy—so even *she* doesn't stink at everything. Convincing yourself that you aren't awful at everything can be tough. It doesn't mean that you should go find someone who is worse than you at certain activities. In fact, you should do just the opposite. If there is someone who does something as poorly as you do, try to identify ways in which that person does something really well. Picking at others (whether in your head or out loud) for being stinky at something isn't going to help their self-esteem or yours. If you can find positive ways others contribute to activities, you can find positive ways you contribute to even the activities you suck at the most.

For example, Nick, who is in your math class, really stinks at algebra. He stays after school for help, does all his homework, studies all evening, and still manages to fail his math tests. Whenever the teacher calls on him, he gets the answer wrong. Does Nick stink at everything? What does he do well? Maybe his strong subject is English, and he hardly has to study to get As. He is persistent. He continues to stay after school and to work hard even though he isn't doing well on math tests. He also puts forth great effort on homework, which earns him some points toward his grade. When the teacher calls on him, even though he is usually wrong, he still tries to answer the question. So does Nick stink at everything? No. Does he stink at math? He struggles with math, but no one could say he's lazy or not trying hard enough. It isn't always easy to find out how you or others contribute to something, but it can be done! Be as kind to yourself in looking for the good as we were to Nick in this example.

 **Reality Check**

Could you actually stink at everything? Find the truth between the extremes and be happy with falling somewhere in the middle. We are going to challenge your beliefs about yourself and make you find some middle ground.

Write down what you believe you stink at:

_____

_____

_____

_____

Do you really stink completely at this? How do you try to improve your stinkiness at this activity?

_____

_____

_____

_____

_____

This is where your focus needs to be, on what you do to not stink—on your efforts and your tiny successes. Imagine how happy Nick would be if he got a D- on a math test instead of an F! Find joy in the little improvements, and you will see that it is silly to judge yourself only with the categories of perfect or horrible. Most people are somewhere in the middle in just about everything—no one is perfect and no one is a total stinker.

## Gray Is the New Black

As a whole, do you have qualities that balance out the things that you don't think you do well? Are you a pretty bad soccer player? Do you struggle with history class? What are your strengths? If you can't think of *anything*, ask people you trust to point out some strengths and write them here. When you are having a particularly bad day thinking you are a stinker, look at this list and use it to help you find a shade of gray. For example, if you are a great dancer, but you just made a moron out of yourself in front of the cool people in school, remind yourself, "I may have been a bit stinky at socializing today, but, man, can I dance!" Finding something positive—related or not to where you believe you stink—can turn your mood around and make the stinky stuff smell a bit sweeter.

Where I Rock:

_____

_____

_____

_____

_____

_____

Cut this list out and carry it in your bag for extra inspiration!

# Chapter 14

## Nobody Likes Me

Some people worry a lot about whether people are mad at them or dislike them, when in fact they might be misreading social cues. Worrying excessively about how others feel about you can make you seem clingy and annoying. The teenage years are a very stressful time. Being liked by the right people at the right time can feel like the most important thing in the world. If someone you want as a friend seems to be angry with you or to dislike you, it can feel like your social life is over. In some unfortunate circumstances, this may affect your social standing.

The most important thing to remember is that your reaction to these types of situations is often more important than the situation itself. If people learn that by snubbing you for one day, you will freak out and do anything to get back in their good graces, they might snub you because it is easy and entertaining to see you freak out. Also, you should be aware that sometimes, when someone snubs you, the snubbing may have nothing to do with you. The person may seem aloof because of something else that is going on in that person's life that is totally unconnected to you.

Have you ever walked down the hall, said "What's up?" to a good friend, and discovered that you are glared at and the greeting isn't returned? Did you worry about what you could have done to upset her until lunchtime, when you saw your friend and she said "Hey" as if nothing had happened? This happens, and you might even be guilty of it at some point. Maybe your friend forgot her contacts and had a migraine headache, so not only did she not see you but also her head hurt so much that she was glaring at everyone. Where you went wrong, however, was in worrying that you did something to cause her reaction, or lack of it, and then spending a lot of time feeling bad and trying to figure out how to fix the situation. You could have just let it go and thought to yourself, "If she has a problem with me, she needs to tell me. Then we can fix it. I can't let it bother me. I have too many other things to think about, like what I am going to do after school, or how I can best prepare for my big biology test."

What a difference! In the first situation, your friend's reaction ruined half of your day for no reason! In the second situation, you pushed her attitude aside, recognized there was nothing you could do about it anyway, and used what little time you had to think about important issues. It isn't easy to push people's reactions out of your mind, but the more practice you have doing it, the better you will be at it.

## The Almighty!

Do I really have so much power over people that my behavior can affect their moods? Probably not! If people are going to be in a snippy mood, they are going to do so whether you did something that bothered them or not. Similar to the Reality Check exercise in Chapter 13, this exercise will teach you new ways to think about people's reactions to you.

**Part 1:** Write down where this person went wrong with her reactions.

**Example:**
Jenn, Heather, and Meaghan are all whispering at the lunch table. When Sheila gets there, they abruptly stop whispering and act kind of rude to her.

Sheila immediately assumes they are saying something mean about her or are leaving her out of something. She is quiet for the rest of the lunch break. For the rest of the day, she feels stressed about what they might have been saying about her. After school, she is still worried, so she calls Tracey, who is friends with Meaghan. She asks her if she knows anything.

Where Sheila went wrong: Immediately assuming they were talking about her; changing the way she acts just because they were acting weird; worrying for the rest of the day; freaking out after school; and involving someone else in the situation.

What would have been a better reaction? Not assuming they were talking about her; even if they were, there was no reason to let it change how she acted for the rest of the day. Sheila would have been better off focusing on school or something positive for the rest of the day. If it was still on her mind after school, she could have asked one of the girls involved instead of making a big mess by talking about it with other people.

**Your turn!**

1. Alicia has four tickets to a popular band's concert. She invites Jenna, Mary, and Eve, but not Joanne. Joanne gets mad right away. She feels that Alicia must not be her real friend; if she were, she would have picked her to go to the concert instead of one of the other girls. Joanne decides to ignore her and the girls she invited to the concert for the rest of the week. She also decides to have a party and not invite any of them.

Where Joanne went wrong _____

_____

_____

_____

_____

What would have been a better reaction? _____

_____

_____

_____

_____

_____

2. Beth didn't wait for Ella before walking to the cafeteria today. Instead, she went to lunch and sat at their regular table. When Ella arrived—late because she had waited for Beth—she was angry to find Beth there. Ella yelled at Beth. She told her she was rude and not to expect her to wait for her tomorrow or ever again. Beth told Ella to shut up; she didn't want her waiting for her anyway. She just wanted everyone to leave her alone.

Where Ella went wrong _____

_____

_____

_____

_____

_____

What would have been a better reaction? _____

_____

_____

_____

_____

_____

_____

**Part 2:** Let's take a look at the culprits in these cases, Alicia and Beth. Why might they have acted the way they did? Maybe Alicia took Joanne to the last concert she went to, and she felt that she should take different people this time? Maybe Beth failed the math test she knew Ella did really well on and she didn't want to be around her until she got over her disappointment over failing the test.

What else could have been going on in their lives to make them act the way they did?

Alicia: _____

\
\
_____

\
\
_____

\
\
_____

Beth: _____

\
\
_____

\
\
_____

\
\
_____

Think about the times you may have acted somewhat unpleasantly to someone or left someone out of a group activity. Was it always because that person did something to you, or were there other things that caused you to make that decision? We generally don't have the almighty power we think we have over everyone around us. Decisions are often made that might affect you but have absolutely nothing to do with you. Try to keep this in mind before you jump to conclusions. Have confidence, and trust that those you care about will let you know if they are being mean or weird because of something you did. Will you get hurt sometimes for no reason? Yes. Everyone does. But you have little control over that. Fretting about something like that all day or beating yourself up because you think you did something to cause it isn't going to fix it; it is only going to stress you out more and do a number on your self-esteem. You can only control yourself, so work on your own reactions. Respect your friends in a way that you would like them to respect you. If they act like jerks or weirdos, brush it off; everyone is allowed an unexplained, jerky day now and then.

# Chapter 15

## Self-Harm

Cutting, burning, picking, and other forms of self-mutilation—these are ways of coping with stress that are unsafe and can become addicting. More and more teenagers are taking part in self-harming behaviors like cutting. The media have focused a lot on these types of behaviors in recent years. This attention is good because it creates awareness and helps people know what resources might be available to help them. But it also is bad because it might give the impression that these behaviors are okay. If you haven't engaged in these harmful behaviors—DON'T! If you've tried one or more of them and hated it, GREAT! Don't do it again. If you have engaged in harmful behaviors in the past, or if you are currently doing something that is self-harming, it is REALLY, REALLY, REALLY important that you talk to someone about it. Find an adult who is trustworthy—like a parent, counselor, doctor, or family friend—and talk to that person.

If you are afraid to tell a parent or guardian, that is a very normal fear. But, unless you have a parent or guardian who is physically or emotionally abusive, this is a person whose job it is to care about you and to make sure that you are safe. If you are hurting yourself, you are not safe. The caring adults in your life need to know that you are feeling this much stress so that they can help you find a better way of dealing with your emotions.

The thought of telling a parent or guardian is probably going to be worse than what happens when that person actually finds out. Hopefully, your parent or guardian will react in a caring and concerned way, and will help you get the assistance you need. But the world is not always so rosy. Your parent or guardian may feel confused, hurt, angry, or scared; we all know how ridiculous adults can act when they are feeling any of these emotions.

If your parent or guardian is scared, he or she might yell at you—"What are you doing that for?!" or, "What are you thinking?! That is stupid. It isn't going to make your problems go away, so knock it off." Oh, or how about this one: "You are grounded if you do it again!" Perhaps your parent or guardian will respond with an annoying, "You're just doing that for attention." And then there is this possibility: "Your life is perfect. We give you everything you could ever want. You can't possibly have that much stress in your life."

Oh, goodness. Adults aren't always without fault. They might pretend that they are, or want you to think that they are, but when they get scared that a child or teenager they care about is hurting and they either didn't see it or don't know how to fix it, they might react like lunatics. Their reaction might be very unhelpful. So what on earth are you supposed to do if you have a feeling your parent or guardian is going to freak out? Well, you can show him this chapter, which he might find very helpful. There is a list of resources included at the end, and that gives some direction as well. If you use this chapter as a way to tell an adult and you aren't sure the adult will know what to do, ask the adult to read the following paragraph:

*The teenager in your life just shared something incredibly difficult with you. No matter what you are feeling, this teenager needs your support more than ever right now and needs to know that you do not think she is a weirdo or freak. She needs a hug and she needs to know that you are going to help her so that she doesn't feel like she is in this alone. You don't have to "cure" her, but you do have to help her get the services she needs. Self-harm is a way of releasing tension and dealing with stress. The teenager in your life is feeling strong emotions and is having a hard time managing them. It is your job as the adult to help her find the help that she needs without freaking out. So pull it together; you can be sad and scared later. Get her to a counselor or doctor who can help you both take care of this situation.*

What do you think? Will that help you tell your parent or guardian what is going on? If not, will it help you tell another adult who can then either tell your parent or guardian for you or help you tell your parent or guardian? I know it is superscary, but going through this alone is overwhelming. Would you try to lift an entire ton of bricks on your own if there were people you could ask for help? What if one of the adults had a forklift and could take most of the burden off you? Wouldn't that be great? Why go it alone if you don't have to? Get someone to help take the load off.

So why is self-harm such a tough thing to stop? For those people who find it helpful, it releases tension, not in a safe way, but for some it is the only way they know to find relief. Unfortunately, once someone starts using this as a coping skill, it is really tough to stop. It can become somewhat addictive and leave people feeling as if there is no other outlet for them when they are feeling stressed. One great way of helping this situation is to learn healthy ways of finding relief that can take the place of these not-so-healthy ways. Included below are a few ways to help you break into the cycle of self-harming behaviors, but for more intense techniques, connecting with a counselor who has experience with these behaviors is best. Reducing stress overall is certainly beneficial, and you will have tons of activities to try in Part III of this book that can help you do that!

 ## STOP IT!

Stopping your habits can be really hard, but it is imperative in situations like this. Breaking into the cycle of addiction is as hard as can be, but it can be done. Learn some techniques to break into this unhealthy cycle.

**Lean on me.** Are you having one of those days where you feel like you need to hurt yourself? Stick by someone all day—like glue. Don't allow yourself to be alone. You don't have to tell people why you are sticking so close; just tell them you need to be with them because you aren't feeling very happy. You are less likely to hurt yourself if you aren't alone.

**Take a break.** Make a deal with yourself. If you feel like hurting yourself, do thirty push-ups, walk around the block, wash your hair, or call two friends. This is a way of distracting yourself from your emotions and will hopefully lower the intensity of the emotions enough so that you can handle them without hurting yourself. Right now, make a list of ways to distract yourself and hang it in your room.

**Lose yourself.** On a happy day, make a mix on your MP3 player, iPod, computer, or wherever you can. The mix can only have songs on it that put you in a happy mood—not sad or depressing songs that make you feel even worse. They must be uplifting. Keep the mix with you wherever you go and listen to it when you feel overwhelmed.

**Drawbacks.** Self-harm might make you feel better for a moment, but does it have drawbacks? List some on a paper that you can keep close to you. Here are some examples: If I have scars on my arms, I can't wear the dress I want to wear for prom. Picking at my skin can lead to infection. I wouldn't want my sister treating her body this way and I want to set a healthy example for her.

Hopefully, these suggestions and other techniques you might learn from someone like a counselor or doctor can help you begin to break the cycle of self-harm.

## Where Can I Go for Help?

This list is for you or the adult you reach out to for help.

1. **Your local emergency room.** Yikes! An emergency room? Doesn't that mean an immediate placement in a psych hospital? No. But if it is three o'clock in the morning, it might be the only place open. They have lists of doctors and counselors they can refer you to who will be able to help. At an ER, you can also have any wounds checked to make sure there are no infections or other dangers.

2. **School counselor, nurse, or teacher.** They are listed in this order for a reason. If you have a guidance counselor or adjustment counselor at school, that person should be knowledgeable about many helpful resources for you and the caring adults in your life to use. He or she may be able to refer you to a counselor or doctor who has experience with self-harm. The nurse can be helpful as well and can check any wounds for infection. If there is no school counselor, the nurse will probably know where to take you for assistance. Teachers can also be great resources; they may not know referral sources, but they should know who in the school can be of assistance.

3. **Primary care physician.** Your primary care physician also should have a list of referrals to people who specialize in self-harm, and he or she can put your mind at ease by checking out any wounds. Many primary care physicians are familiar with self-harm and can really help you feel as though you are not in this alone.

4. **Local emergency team.** Not every city or town has a local emergency team, and it is often difficult to find out where they are or how to contact them. One way of finding out is by contacting the schools in your area, the local hospital, or the police, and asking,

"Does our town or city have an emergency psychiatric team? If so, could I please have the phone number?" These emergency teams are often made up of mental health professionals who can talk to you at a health center, hospital, and sometimes even at your home. They also will assess your safety and provide you with helpful resources.

5. **Health insurance card.** Talk to your parent or guardian about whether you may have health insurance coverage that might cover the resources such as a counselor or physician you may wish to use. Have them help you work with the provider to determine your health insurance coverage.

# Chapter 16

## The Fancy Terms

There are no exercises in this chapter. It is just an overview, in regular terms, of some clinical terms related to anxiety that you might hear thrown around. We also will go over definitions of specific phobias and discuss some helpful resources. Now, when you look at these definitions, remember, they are basic definitions. If you think some of the descriptions sound like you, keep them in mind, but don't fret about them! None of these terms mean that you or anyone who might fit into the definition is crazy. This is simply meant to help you figure out what some of the clinical terms mean. It is not meant to diagnose you or to help you diagnose your friends. Only a professional can do that. If you do have a diagnosis, or if you are afraid that you will be diagnosed, relax. The word "diagnosis" is a little scary, but the important thing about being diagnosed is that it helps the people who are helping you figure out what they need to do to make you feel better. Did you know that cars get diagnosed? If your car is making a strange noise, when you take it in to the shop, a mechanic will diagnose it—figure out what the noise is, why it is happening, and how to fix it. Only then will the mechanic fix it. So, if you have a diagnosis or are afraid you will receive one, try to think of yourself as a car going in for a tune-up. We all could use a tune-up at some point.

### Common Symptom Terms

**Palpitations.** This word is used to describe a feeling many people get in their hearts when it feels as though it is beating differently than normal. People who describe having heart palpitations might also feel like their heart is pounding, skipping beats, going faster than usual, or just doesn't feel right.

**Compulsion.** This is when you feel like you *must* do a certain act or repetitive motion. If you don't do it, your anxiety might feel worse. Think about the rituals and superstitious things many people do before playing sports or taking a test. These can be described as compulsions for many people, and the feeling that they must do it is the compulsion.

**Obsessions.** These are thoughts that intrude upon your mind whether you want to think about them or not, so when they get in your head, they cause distress. If you try really hard not to think about something, if it is an obsession, it usually bullies its way right into your head. Obsessions and compulsions are buddies and the two combined can create obsessive-compulsive tendencies or obsessive-compulsive disorder.

**Hypervigilance.** This is being superaware of what is going on around you. People who act hypervigilant often seem on edge or jumpy in certain situations. They are usually quite alert about their surroundings, but being so on edge can often tire them out.

**Dissociation.** This can feel like having an out-of-body experience in some ways. It is almost as if you are not really in the moment, but observing, or *really* spaced out. There are many different levels of dissociation; some people just feel removed from a situation, while others may have little recollection that they took part in it.

**Paresthesia.** This is a fancy name for numbness or tingling sensations in your body.

**Diaphoretic.** This is another fancy name; this one means sweaty. When you are superanxious and you sweat because of how you are feeling, you might hear a health professional say, "She is diaphoretic."

## Specific Phobias and Anxieties

The following list is not exhaustive and, again, it is not intended for you to use to diagnose yourself or your friends. These definitions are meant to be simplified versions of the clinical ones health professionals use.

**Generalized anxiety disorder.** This one stinks because it is quite general and can affect you in many aspects of your life. It often is an overwhelming feeling of anxiety most of the time, which lasts for at least six months.

**Agoraphobia.** The root of this word is really the fear of going to a marketplace. If you look into ancient Greek history, *agora* was the word for marketplace. People with agoraphobia often fear leaving the house to go to crowded places like malls, stores, or concerts.

**Panic disorder.** There are different types of panic disorders. Some people have panic attacks when they have to do something they are already afraid to do, and some have panic attacks that are totally out of the blue.

**Post-traumatic stress disorder (PTSD).** This term gets thrown around a lot in day-to-day conversation. If you were horribly embarrassed or scared by something, you might say, "I have total PTSD over that." If you do have PTSD, then you had to have experienced a trauma in which you feared your life, body, or health was in grave danger. Since then, you have had a variety of symptoms, such as not being able to stop thinking about the experience, trouble sleeping, hypervigilance, or avoiding situations. There are many more possible symptoms, but this is a general idea of PTSD.

**Obsessive-compulsive disorder (OCD).** This is another term we often use in daily conversation. If someone is meticulous or particular about cleanliness or about how things look, we might say, "He is utterly OCD about his desk." He may be, but if so, not having his desk the way he likes it would make him extremely anxious and uncomfortable, and it wouldn't be funny at all to him if his desk were out of order. OCD takes up *a lot* of time for those who deal with it, because their minds are constantly overrun by the obsessions and then they feel compelled to take part in some sort of repetitive action.

**Trichotillomania.** This is a fun word to say, and a very interesting disorder. Sometimes people with anxiety pull their hair out—the hair on their heads, eyelashes, eyebrows, arms, wherever! Unfortunately it can lead to bald patches, but the compulsion to pull out the hair is so strong that the consequences don't really matter to the person doing it.

## Specific Phobias

These are fears about something specific; they occur even though the person who has the fear knows it is unreasonable. They are extremely annoying because those dealing with them know that they shouldn't be so afraid, but they can't seem to help themselves. Imagine seeing a teeny tiny spider and almost fainting. That is what can happen to people with arachnophobia—the fear of spiders. Chances are you can just stomp on the spider and any danger would be gone, but someone with arachnophobia would be too scared to approach the spider to step on it.

The following are some common specific phobias.

**Animal type.** This would include arachnophobia and is a fear of an animal or insect.

**Natural environment type.** This would include fear of storms, heights, water, or any part of the natural environment.

**Blood-injection-injury type.** This is used to describe those who are afraid of seeing blood, giving blood, getting shots, or undergoing other invasive medical procedures.

**Situational type.** This kind of specific phobia is very common and includes fear of flying (very common), driving, being in a tunnel, public transportation, elevators, and other defined situations.

That was a quick description of some clinical terms related to anxiety. If any of the terms made you at all anxious, have a look at the following helpful resources:

**http://kidshealth.org/teen.** This is an awesome website that is geared strictly to teens and even has tips on how to talk to your parents about things like anxiety. They cover many topics, including anxiety.

**www.bostonleah.org.** This website is run by the very knowledgeable folks at Boston Children's Hospital and has tips for teens, their families, and for health professionals.

**http://mentalhealth.samhsa.gov.** This website might look a little overwhelming because it includes so much information, but you can actually type in your zip code to find resources in your community. It also has great information about substance abuse and mental health for all ages, and is part of the Substance Abuse and Mental Health Services Administration website.

**www.nimh.nih.gov/health/topics/anxiety-disorders/index.shtml.** This is another OMG site, because it has so much information. You could look at this website for hours, but if you go right to the anxiety disorders section, which is the one listed, you will find cool stuff to read and another way of finding a health professional near you who works with anxiety disorders. This is part of the National Institute of Mental Health website.

**www.activeminds.org.** This group is supercool. They run programs designed to help take the stigma out of having a mental health issue. Their Frequently Asked Questions (FAQ) section rocks—it helps you help friends, ask for help, find help, and so on. It also has a section called "Getting Help," which lists toll free numbers you can call for resources in your area.

**www.copecaredeal.org.** This website has helpful tips on coping skills, reaching out for help, and dealing with a diagnosis. It also has a great list of resources you can link to, such as the Anxiety Disorders Association of America and many others.

# Part III

## Deal with It!

Learn techniques that can help minor things that stress you out as well as overwhelming anxieties. The next chapters will go over specific proven techniques that can help even the coolest cucumber.

# Chapter 17

## You Are Freakin' Awesome

Say this out loud: "I am freakin' awesome." You need to believe you are, because on days when you don't think anyone believes you rock, you are the only one who can convince yourself otherwise. This chapter will help you boost your self-esteem and have the pleasant side effect of breaking down some of the anxiety you may feel.

Ever have a day when you felt like you had no friends? Maybe people are being mean to you, not including you, or ousting you for some reason?

Days like that are horrible; as a teenage girl, you are bound to have one if not many. Teenage girls can be pretty cruel and leave each other out of social situations—perhaps to make themselves feel more powerful or popular. Sometimes they tease and make fun of someone, which can really ruin that person's day, month, or year. At times it comes without any instigation on your part, but just in case, double-check your own behavior: Are you being cruel or catty? Did you hurt someone's feelings? If so, make amends, be the bigger person, and put an end to the drama. If you are innocent, or if people continue to be cruel after you have done your best to remedy the situation, remember that you still have control over how you react to being the odd one out or the target of teasing.

You have heard it before, and you will hear it again: ignore them. Okay, admittedly, it's much easier said than done. If it were so easy to ignore, it wouldn't make you wish the cafeteria floor would swallow you whole, or that you could switch schools to get away. But seriously, at least pretend to ignore them. If people are saying cruel things about you, every single time you hear something negative about yourself, write down a positive word, or a positive aspect about yourself. It doesn't have to be anything major; it can be anything: my toes are wicked cute; I am good at math; I can burp like nobody's business. Find something and write it down. If you don't want to write a full sentence, write a word that makes you feel happy—toes, math, burp. That way, no one will have a clue what you are writing. Then, find someone—anyone—and say something nice to her. If you see the nurse in the hallway, tell her that her hair looks nice. If you see your neighbor raking leaves, tell her that she is doing a great job. If you see a nervous freshman in the hallway, smile and say, "Hi." For every negative comment you hear, identify something positive about yourself, and say something positive to someone else. Voilà! Instant happiness, right? Not quite.

If life continues to stink, and people are being nasty for no reason, school, social situations, group gatherings, and other circumstances can become overwhelming and anxiety provoking. But if you decide to stop participating in activities because other people are making you feel lousy, then you are only giving them what they want and the only one who loses out is you. You will feel superlousy when you miss out on something. So stay involved. Don't let other people's jerkiness prevent you from participating. Look at the words or sentences you wrote down when they said mean things. Keep them in your head as you walk into whatever situation makes you anxious. These words are like shields and will help you deflect any negative things people are saying. Still feel anxious? Think about all the positive things you have done every time they do something negative. What a nice way to counteract their negative influence on the universe. You are filling it with positive energy. Still feel crappy? Well, pretend you don't, hold your chin up, and know that you are doing the best you can. If they are still cruel, then it is a huge relief that they aren't your friends. Who would want to be friends with people who can make someone feel so awful?

Still feel awful? Try the following activities and see if they help you recognize how awesome you are and how little someone else's opinion of you matters. These people are very unlikely to be around you in twenty years to make you feel horrible. But *you* will be around you, so learn to take care of yourself. Be nice to yourself; find ways to remind yourself that you are great and have many accomplishments that no one can take away. If the present looks bleak, focus on the future and the dreams you have for yourself that certainly don't include these meanies.

The preceding suggestions can also work in situations where you feel anxious for no good reason. Every time you worry about an activity you have to do, write down a positive word or sentence, and then give someone a compliment for doing a good job at something. If you are about to enter into an anxiety-provoking situation, think of all those positive words, people you have seen be successful at things, and go for it. The following activities will also help you build up your self-esteem and show you that you can do it—no matter what "it" may be. It just may be that you take a little longer, approach things differently, or require a little help from a friend.

## Who Am I Anyway?

Who do you want to be? How do you want people to see you? Remember the collage from Chapter 9? Take it out and get ready to make it even cooler. If you made a shoebox with that activity, you are going to start filling up the box with even more inspiration. Think of this shoebox as a self-esteem "I Am Awesome" toolbox. Find pictures in magazines, photo albums, or on the Web that represent how you want to be seen by others. Now, using copies of pictures of yourself, glue your face onto the pictures you have cut out. Do you think Michelle Obama has great fashion sense? Cut out a picture of her and put your face where hers is! Now staple that to your collage or put it in your toolbox. Is your cousin Andrea nice to everyone, even the relatives who drive you crazy? Cut out a picture of her to inspire your own kindness and add it to your collage or toolbox. Look at your creation anytime you feel you need a boost in self-esteem. Another cool thing about this is you can change it as much as you want. No longer wish to dress like Michelle Obama, but instead want to be a doctor in scrubs? Cut out a picture of a doctor and paste your face right on it!

If you want to get supercreative, do this activity with a friend and make a photo studio in your room or outside. Create a photo shoot based on how you want others to see you and, more important, who you want to be. Have fun with it. Find a way to dress up as a pilot or to stage a fashion show. Feel self-conscious in front of the camera? Stay behind it and take pictures of others doing a job or task you would like to do. Find inspiration and click away. Print the pictures and either add them to your collage or place them in your toolbox. Look at them at least once a week for inspiration; remember, you can change them whenever you want.

### ✎ Personal Best

Pick an activity you are really bad at and improve upon it! If you are awful at running, challenge yourself. Can you run five minutes this week and six minutes next week? Finding something you can improve upon without the added stress of others' expectations can be great for your self-esteem. So often we expect to be perfect. When we are good at something, others often expect a great deal from us. One way to boost your self-esteem is to improve upon something you are actually pretty bad at without major expectations from yourself or anyone else. If you decide to try running, the goal isn't to become the best on the track team, the goal is to see if you can run five minutes instead of four and that is a huge accomplishment! Use the example below as a guideline and then fill out your own personal best worksheet:

Pick an activity you are bad at, but don't really care that you aren't a rock star at it.

**Activity:** . . . . . *Running*

Now set an achievable goal—set it low to begin with and see how it goes. Remember, don't feel pressure; this is just for fun.

**Goal:** . . . . . . . . *Run for twenty minutes without stopping, or keeling over.*

Now go for it! Keep track of how you are working toward your goal; remember any progress toward your goal is awesome. There is no time limit.

**Week 1:** . . . . . . *I ran around the block twice this week! Each time took four minutes.*

**Week 2:** . . . . . . *I ran around the block one and a half times on Monday and once on Wednesday. I am a superwoman!*

Continue like this until you reach your goal. Then make yourself an award, take yourself out for a manicure, or just enjoy your personal accomplishment. The best thing about it is that you did it, and NO ONE can ever take it away from you. It is all yours.

## Personal Best Worksheet

Activity: _____

_____

Goal: _____

_____

    Check it: Are you aiming too high? Remember, don't put yourself under any pressure!

    Progress Checks (Slow and steady wins the race. You don't even have to win anything, so go as slow as you need!)

Week 1: _____

_____

Week 2: _____

_____

Week 3: _____

_____

Week 4: _____

_____

Week 5: _____

_____

Week 6: _____

_____

Are you closer to your goal? Or did you make your goal already? No matter what, six weeks is a long time to stick to something. Give yourself kudos for being awesome!

# Chapter 18

## Talk to Myself?

Everyone already thinks I'm crazy; now, they'll *know* I am! Yes, this chapter works on positive self-talk and reality-testing self-talk. Although it sounds cheesy and wacky, it can help immensely! And everyone is wacky; it is just that some people are in denial and some people have accepted it. The sooner you accept your own quirkiness, the sooner you will love yourself more for it. Imagine if we were all totally normal? That would be incredibly boring, so get ready to talk to yourself!

Okay, so in public you don't have to talk out loud to yourself, but you can talk to yourself in your head without moving your lips or pretending to be a ventriloquist. Positive self-talk is when you take what you are anxious about or feeling not so hot about and pump yourself up about it. You become your own coach and give yourself a pep talk. It is pretty similar to finding things about yourself that make you awesome; now, you just have to say it to yourself and really pump it up. For example, if you have horrible social anxiety but really want to go to a party, practicing positive self-talk may help.

Prior to going to the party, look in the mirror—make sure your door is locked so that no snoopy sibling will point at you and laugh—and say your version of "I am going to go to this party and have fun. I know I get anxious, but I really want to have a social life and this party is important to me. If I get nervous at the party, I can find a friend, step outside, or pretend to text on my cell phone. I can do this." When you do this, make sure you talk about wanting to go to the event, why it could be fun, and also accept your anxiety. It is there, so acknowledge it. Once you say "hi" to it, you can also say "good-bye" to it!

Okay, that is the most embarrassing part of positive self-talk, and it isn't so bad. If you are really anxious, however, Negative Nelly might come out and try to beat down Positive Petunia. Both Nelly and Petunia live in your head, so tune into Petunia and tune out Nelly. Funny thing is, you have control over both Nelly and Petunia, so focus on Petunia and help her out! Here is an example of how this might go—and this can happen while looking in the mirror, while heading to the party, or while at the party.

P: This party is going to be fun, I am—

N: [Cackling] No, it won't be, you big loser. Everyone else will have fun, but no one is going to talk to you.

P: Go away, Negative Nelly. That's not true. Jessica is going to be there and I'm sure we'll have fun.

N: *Mmmm.* I don't think so. Jessica likes Rob, and he's going to be there, so she'll drop you like a hot potato if he decides he wants to hang with her.

P: Well, that might be true, but she's a good friend and I don't think she'll do that. Plus, I have plenty of other friends and—

N: No, you don't. You are totally lame and your hair looks like crap. You should probably just stay home.

P: NO! I'm going to the party. My palms are sweating and I am nervous, but I am not lame. I have many good qualities and people like me whether or not I'm having a good hair day. I'm going to go to the party and I'm going to have a good time.

N: Don't say I didn't warn you . . .

P: You are wrong, Negative Nelly. I'm strong and awesome and I'm going to the party!

Yes, you have to fight for Positive Petunia. She is going to get you to that party and help you keep your chin up even if the party stinks. You have to fight the negative voices. Sometimes, the Negative Nellys will win, but the harder you fight them, the more prepared you will be to fight them in the future and the less energy it will take to win. So if you try this and it doesn't work the first time, try again and keep trying until it works, because it will.

Hand in hand with positive self-talk comes reality-testing self-talk. They are really intertwined, but reality-testing self-talk uses proof from past experiences to fight feelings of "I can't do this, I stink at this, I honk." So for reality-testing self-talk, you need to have some experience under your belt. Say, for example, Tabitha has performance anxiety and is supposed to play a solo on her saxophone in an upcoming concert. She has performed before. Some of her performances went well, and others she totally tanked. How could she boost her self-confidence about her upcoming performance? Enter Negative Nelly and Positive Petunia:

P:   Okay, I can do this. I love the saxophone and it is an honor to have a solo.

N:   Maybe an honor for you, but not for those who have to hear you! Remember last time when you totally stunk and the saxophone made that awful noise?

P:   Yes, I do. It was awful in the moment, but no one really remembers it now and I still got up there and gave it my best. Plus, the performance before that was great!

N:   Everyone gets lucky once. You stink.

P:   No, I don't. I am first chair in saxophone, I won the state competition, and my teacher only picks people for solos that he thinks can do a good job.

N:   He probably only picked you for some laughs or because he feels bad for you. You are awful at performing in public.

P:   I've practiced well all week, and I've performed well in the past. I know I can perform well. If for some reason I don't, I will know I tried my hardest and the people who care about me will continue to care about me regardless of how my performance goes. But, I'm going to rock it.

N:   I don't—

P:   Be quiet, Nelly! This is going to be great, so shut up!

Be as pleasant or as unpleasant as you must be with Nelly, but do shut her up and go out and rock it!

 ## No Negative Nastiness

Challenge your negative self-talk with positive self-talk and change your beliefs about yourself. This also can work if there is someone in your life who says negative things to you or about you. Challenge what they say with your own positive self-talk and suck the *oomph* right out of their words.

Is there something you often say to yourself to beat yourself up? Write it down below. Is there something a parent, friend, teacher, or anyone else has said to you that really bothers you or makes you feel less confident? Write that down below as well. Now, turn negative sayings into positive sayings, like in the example:

## Negative

*My English teacher said, "I hope you don't plan on studying English in college. You're a horrible writer."*

## Positive

*I enjoy my writing and writing is so subjective that someone else might think it is great!*

_____

_____

_____

_____

# Chapter 19

## One Step at a Time

A great way to stop feeling overwhelmed is by breaking large tasks into smaller ones. You can learn to organize your book bag, social life, room (this will please your parent or guardian too!), and more. Organization can be a royal pain in the you-know-what, but once you have a system to follow, it can really decrease your anxiety. The most important part about organizing things is that it needs to be done in a way that is helpful to *you* and that *you* understand. What works for one person doesn't always work for another. For example, if your mom color-codes everything, that doesn't mean that her color codes will mean anything to you—you might prefer to alphabetize things. Whatever method will help you feel more organized is what you should use.

One annoying part about organization is that you usually don't realize you're unorganized until a situation is chaotic and even thinking about organizing it is totally overwhelming. Please keep in mind that your messes weren't created in a day; realistically, they won't get organized in a day, so tackle disarray piece by piece. Make a deal with yourself that you will work on organizing something for thirty minutes a day, or work on a specific area until it is done. *Do not* try to tackle everything at once. It will probably just make you anxious. Once you see that you can accomplish some organization in a little time, the rest won't look quite so bad!

Another key aspect to organization is that you have to keep at it; this is the annoying part. Taking a Saturday to get everything organized is great, but if you don't keep up with it, it will just become unorganized again. So, you will have to set aside some time on at least a weekly basis for the pieces of your life that you would like to keep organized. For some, this is where they slack. After a day of school, playing basketball, doing homework, and helping out around the house, the last thing you want to do is spend time straightening up your room or organizing your homework. If you put it off, however, you might find that you keep putting it off and, before you know it, you are totally unorganized, can't find things you need (causing great anxiety), and then must spend a weekend feeling overwhelmed by a mountain of chaos you have to reorganize. Staying on top of it really will help. If you can commit to a little time each week, you will save yourself stress and anxiety, and free up any days you would have spent reorganizing!

## ✎ Score!!!

Achieving goals is much easier if you actually tend to that goal instead of just going for it with no road map. If you break down your goals into achievable steps, the task will be less overwhelming and you will have a method to your madness. Let's tackle your schoolbag as an example, and then you can tackle the task of your choice following some simple steps.

You look in your schoolbag and see crumpled papers (maybe that's my missing math homework), messy notebooks (hmm, I don't even want to open those they look so bad), gum (would have been nice to chew some of that after eating garlic bread with Joe), loose change (hey, I *did* have enough to buy that soda the other day), pens galore (oops, I knew I had one in here; oh wait, there are like fifteen . . .), keys to the house (so much for the new set I had to pay for), and who knows what else! If your schoolbag — or any part of your life—looks like that, it's a wonder you can find anything. Looking for things without any pressure is one thing, but when you need to hand in homework ASAP, or need to pee but you are searching for your house keys, every second counts, and every millisecond that goes by brings more and more anxiety. This makes it hard to focus and nearly impossible to find what you are seeking. So let's get organized. That schoolbag might be overwhelming when you look in it, so let's set our goal and break it down. First things first: what is our goal? We need to organize that schoolbag!

**Goal:** Organize schoolbag so that I can find stuff in it.

> *How can I start organizing it without even seeing what is in it? Good point . . .*

**Step 1:** Dump out schoolbag onto a clean surface where no little siblings or pets will try to eat or steal any contents.

*OMG—there is so much crap! It would be a lot easier to stuff it back in there…but then I will still be unorganized. Maybe I should separate everything into piles of similar things…*

**Step 2:** Put everything that is related to each other in piles—writing utensils in one pile, gum and mints in another, technological devices in another, papers in another, and so on.

*Yikes. I have like thirty piles. Well, it is better than the one pile I started out with; maybe I should tackle each pile on its own.*

**Step 3:** Go through the individual piles and see what I really need in my schoolbag, what I can toss, and what belongs somewhere else.

*I still have a billion piles, but now I can throw these ones out, put the stuff that belongs elsewhere on my desk to tackle later, and stay focused on my schoolbag.*

**\*VERY IMPORTANT**

**Don't get distracted by putting away the piles of stuff that go elsewhere. You are here to focus on your goal of organizing your schoolbag. The other stuff can wait!**

**Step 4:** Now you only have the piles that belong in your schoolbag left to tackle. Is there a way that you can organize these to fit in your bag so that you know where they are? Separate all these items into piles, depending on where you will situate them in your bag.

*Hmmm. All my notebooks and papers should probably go in the big pocket of my schoolbag. I can never find my keys when I put them in the big pocket, so maybe those should go with my cell phone, mints, and change in the little pocket. There is really no place for my pens. I guess I can throw them back in the big pocket.*

**Step 5:** Do these piles make sense? Should you do some organizing within the piles? Look to make sure you will truly be putting things away so that you can get to them with ease.

*This is helpful, but my change will still be all over the place. I guess I could put my change in a little pouch or bag. Oooh, I could put an elastic around my pens so they are at least all together. I also could put all my loose papers in a folder.*

**Step 6:** Put it all back in your bag and go for a trial run. Do you need a pen? Where is it? Is your cell phone ringing? Can you find it easily? Tweak the organization if you find you are struggling.

**Step 7:** Stay on top of it! Give it a quick look every day and make sure change isn't being tossed in the big pocket or that pens aren't rolling around haphazardly.

Now you try!

**Goal:** What do you want to accomplish? Pick something specific, *not* "I am going to organize my whole life!"

**Step 1:** Look at the whole picture without any distractions.

**Step 2:** Break the task into piles of similar items or sections (if you are tackling a room, section by section is helpful).

**Step 3:** Where does this belong? Here? Trash? Elsewhere? Divvy it up and toss what needs to be tossed and put the "Elsewhere" pile elsewhere! Focus on the "Here" pile! You can deal with the "Elsewhere" pile later.

**Step 4:** Reorganize the "Here" pile into piles that belong together as far as where you will put them.

**Step 5:** Do these piles make sense? Can I organize within this pile to make it even more organized?

**Step 6:** Put it all away. Step back and take a look: Does it make sense? Do I like it? Change anything that isn't working for you.

**Step 7:** Keep up with it! Dedicate a few minutes a day to putting things in their places.

## Calendars Are Key

Social planning, sports planning, school planning—believe it or not, keeping a daily planner is really tough for some people and finding the perfect system to keep you organized can take some time. How do you stay organized now? Do you like written lists, alarms on your cell phone, or huge spreadsheets? Do you like to check things off, cross things out, or highlight them when they are done? Do you hope you remember what you are supposed to do and where you are supposed to be? There are many different ways to set up a calendar or to-do list, and just like organizing, what works can be totally different for everyone.

This exercise is a trial-and-error one, so you can keep trying things until they work for you. You may use the examples here for inspiration or come up with something that is totally your own. Below is a description of common tools for planning. For free calendars on the Internet go to www.calendars thatwork.com.

## Types of Calendars

**Daily calendars:** These calendars have a good amount of space to write in for each day, but you might only see one to two days on a page. If you think you will be writing a bunch of stuff for each day—like someone's birthday, homework assignments, practice schedule, and chores—this might be the right calendar for you.

**Weekly calendars:** Looking at your schedule for the week can be helpful if you aren't going to be writing as much per day. You would likely be able to fit in a work schedule, birthdays, events, and after-school activities, but stuff like homework and chores might need their own to-do list or separate notebook. If you like to have an idea of your whereabouts for the week but don't feel as though you need your whole to-do list on the same page, this might work for you.

**Monthly calendars:** Looking at your schedule for the month can be particularly helpful if you have a lot of events to remember and you need to schedule things around those events. The space to write here is small, so you can probably fit events and one or two schedules (work and practice) in, but even that might be a lot. If you are someone who likes to look ahead, this might be your best choice.

## To-Do Lists

Now, keeping a to-do list seems like a very simple idea, but it isn't for everyone. You may decide you need a checklist for homework and a cross-off list for chores. Whatever you decide, don't make yourself list crazy and have a million lists that you can't keep track of—that will just make you feel more overwhelmed and this is what we are trying to avoid! You might choose different styles for different activities, but keep them all on one page or in one area you can easily access. One fun hint for to-do lists: if you are feeling especially down on yourself for not accomplishing much one day, look back at your day and write down what you *did* accomplish, then check these things off, and you will feel quite productive (put whatever you want on there—get out of bed, brush teeth, comb hair).

The first step is to determine how you will write your list: Straightforward, Prioritized, or Color Coded.

**Straightforward:** As you learn you need to do things, you write them down in a list. There is no priority to any one item; you just have a to-do list that includes everything you need to do.

**Prioritized:** Some things may be more imperative to get done than others. If so, you might put a number one, or a symbol of some sort next to those important items. You may also put them first on your to-do list, and anything that isn't quite as important can go to the bottom.

**Color Coded:** You might be keeping track of a bunch of to-dos for different areas of your life. You could then pick colors to represent the different areas. Everything school related could be written or highlighted in blue, home could be red, and so forth. Also, you could use color-coding to help prioritize—important things in red, less important in blue, and so on!

Your second step, now that you know how you are going to write down what you need to get done, is to decide how you are going to keep track of what you accomplished.

**Reminder only:** For this one, your to-do list is simply a reminder list and as you finish the items on the list, you leave the list as is.

**Checklists:** As silly as it may sound, having a box to check off when you accomplish something can feel awesome! Decide if you want your check box on the left or the right of the task you need to accomplish and get checking.

**Cross-off lists:** Drawing a big black line through something you had to get done can take your anxiety away. Just make sure the line you draw isn't too thick; it is helpful to be able to read the task you accomplished even after you finished it.

## Techno-Savvy Organizing

There are so many cool technological devices out there that can help with organization. The problem with them is the technology: if your battery dies, you can't get on the Internet, or if any sort of technical glitch occurs, you might be in deep doodoo unless you backed up your calendar or to-do list. That is why some of us old-timers appreciate some techie tools but stick to paper and pencil for other things!

**Cell phones:** Cell phones used to be for talking. Now they play music, have alarms, calendars, places for notes, and even take pictures! If you always have your cell phone with you, keeping your calendar and any to-do items in your phone could work well for you. If you are often late, or lose track of time easily, a cell phone might also be your best bet because you can set an alarm to go off prior to needing to be somewhere or to remind you to get something done at a certain time.

**Web calendars:** These are so cool and can really be helpful if your family has a lot of people doing different things each day. You might put your work schedule in the calendar, your sister might have her soccer schedule in there, and your mom can add in her business trip schedule. That way, anyone in the family can access the calendar and it can help everyone figure out who is where, when everyone is free for dinner, when someone needs a ride, etc. They are pretty neat and useful. Some cool ones to try include Outlook, iCal, Microsoft Entourage, and Google Calendar. You can also buy software at many office supply stores.

**PDAs:** PDA stands for personal digital assistant (not public display of affection in this case!). These may be obsolete with all of the advances that have been made in cell phone technology. PDAs are set up like computerized handheld daily planners. You can create calendars, to-do lists, notes, and alarms. Usually you can link them to your computer to back up any information, and many are capable of e-mail. They were once all the rage, but with cell phones being so prevalent, you may be able to do all of this through your cell phone instead.

Now that you have some suggestions, try them out and see which ones work best for you!

# Chapter 20

## Down to Earth

When anxious thoughts and feelings run amok, just finding the ground beneath your feet can be difficult. Have you ever had an overwhelming feeling of anxiety where your body started to feel really strange and you felt like you were going to have a major anxiety attack or out-of-body experience? One way to get back to the here and now is to try a relaxation technique known as grounding. During grounding, you focus on bringing yourself out of feelings of panic and back into the present. Grounding will help you recognize that you are safe and have some control over your body. For example, if you begin to feel panicky, stop and find something concrete—like the ground. Say to yourself (in your head), "The ground is beneath my feet. It is supporting me. I am standing on the ground and I am okay." What else around you is safe? "I am with Janice. She is right next to me and she is feeling fine. There is no need to worry." With grounding, you are really just pointing out the facts so that you can focus on them instead of on your nerves. The ground is there, your friend is there, and you are safe. It sounds silly and stupid, but have you ever seen someone get off a plane after a rough flight? Many people kiss the ground. People who do this literally feel better once they feel the safety of the ground underneath them. Kissing the ground only proves to their bodies and minds that the ground is really there; they are safe now.

If you need to feel more stable, like the folks getting off the plane, you also can touch something to ground yourself. If anxiety makes you dizzy, touching a sturdy wall or piece of furniture can help while you remind yourself, "This is a wall. It can hold me up, and it will not let me fall."

Grounding techniques are often used for people who have fears related to a past trauma or phobias such as social phobias or fear of public speaking.

If you have experienced a trauma, you might have a flashback of the event or experience something that triggers a memory of the event. Grounding can help you come back to the present when you focus on the concrete things around you and not the emotions from the past. Try out the following grounding techniques to see if they help you manage your anxiety.

## Sense Brings Sensibility

Our senses sometimes bring on anxiety, but they also can bring on relaxation. Grounding can be difficult at times if you have a hard time finding concrete items that make you feel safe or calm. So, we are going to find five different things that you can take with you anywhere in order to help you stay grounded. They involve most of the five senses. We are going to leave the sense of taste out because if you turn to cookie dough ice cream for relaxation every time you feel anxious, you are going to develop another problem—food addiction. We are going to work with "safer" senses: smell, touch, sound, sight, and movement. Movement isn't really a sense, but for this exercise, we will pretend that it is!

**Smell:** Did you know that our sense of smell is incredible when it comes to memory? Our memories are often triggered by a scent. Is there a scent you relate to happiness or relaxation? Maybe your grandfather's cologne? Your mom's apple pie? Coffee from your favorite coffee shop? Find a scent and figure out how to take it with you. If it is a perfume, you can usually get a sample size. If it is almost any food or floral scent, you are almost sure to find a similar scent in a candle. They make little candles that you can easily throw into your purse. If you start to feel anxious, excuse yourself for a moment and take a whiff of your calming scent. While you sniff, let the anxiety from your day disappear and be replaced by the calm that this scent brings. Close your eyes and imagine yourself surrounded by this scent. Let the rest of the world disappear for a few minutes while you breathe in the relaxation. Weird, right? But usually quite effective!!

**Touch:** Have you ever known someone who carries a smooth rock or a carved piece of wood as a lucky charm? Often, to bring on good luck, people will rub the rock or piece of wood. The rubbing motion can also be very calming for people. Is there a certain texture you like? A smooth stone? A piece of satin? A soft fabric? These can also be carried around easily in your pocket or purse. Maybe you will choose a piece of satin because it reminds you of the blanket you had as a little kid. Rubbing it between your fingers can bring a sense of calm that you felt as a youngster. Find something that suits your fancy and keep it on (or in) hand.

**Sound:** Okay, this one you can't do in as many places as smell and touch because you need to be able to listen to a sound of your choice on a CD or MP3 player. If you are a music buff, pick out music that helps you relax—not music that makes you cry or makes you angry, but gentle music that makes you feel at peace. You might also try listening to sounds of the ocean, a rainstorm, or some other sound that is soothing to you. Make a mix that you can listen to prior to an anxiety-provoking event. Let the music keep you calm and soothe you so that you enter the situation in a chilled-out state. Keep the music playing in your head if you can't take your music or sounds with you. Let the music keep you calm and override your anxiety.

**Sight:** This is a fun one because it involves finding a picture that either reminds you of a time when you felt totally relaxed or looks like a place that would be relaxing. Pictures of beaches, forests, or mountains are often very peaceful. Take the picture with you and look at it for calming inspiration wherever you go. Imagine yourself immersed in that picture and let yourself go there instead of into the emotions of anxiety.

**Movement:** This one isn't always as discreet as the others, but it can be incredibly effective. Find a slight movement that reminds you to relax. One great one is shrugging your shoulders way up to your ears, making them as tense as possible, and then dropping them down and feeling them relax. Do this a few times and feel the relaxation it brings. Now let the relaxation from your shoulders trickle down to your toes. This minimal movement should work in the short term until you can really move your body in a yoga class, stretching class, or by going for a run.

Each of these five "senses" is a way of grounding yourself. You are taking yourself out of the emotion of anxiety and into a calm place by using any one of these five. These five items can travel anywhere with you, so pack a calming bag of relaxation and beat down that anxiety!

# Chapter 21

## Out of Sight, Out of Mind

Mindfulness, or being present for the task or experience you are doing, is a great way to relieve anxiety. If you can learn to concentrate on the one activity that is in front of you instead of on everything that you need to do, should do, did do, or could have done, it can greatly diminish anxiety. It is not easy to be mindful. We live in a multitasking society. We have constant input coming into our brains while we are trying to form output and retain important information. It's crazy—no wonder our world is so filled with anxiety! Have you ever tried to get ready for an event in a hurry, only to find that by the time you leave, you forgot the one item you needed to bring? While you were getting ready, you were probably thinking something along the lines of, "Shoot! I am so late! Hunter is going to kill me. If I'm late, I won't get a seat. Oh, wait, did I unplug that curling iron? Does this dress even look right? I should have started my day earlier and showered before my brother. Being late stinks…"

Thoughts such as this might be going through your head while you are brushing your teeth, listening to the radio, and texting your friend to save you a seat. All of this clogs up your brain so that you can't really focus on the task at hand. The distraction of your mind chatter can cause significant anxiety. If you can just focus on one task at a time, that one task would probably get done faster and without mistakes; you would also feel a lot calmer and more relaxed while doing it. Focusing on the task in front of you is pretty tough in today's world, but it can be so helpful that it is worth practicing.

## ✎ Wash the Dishes

Who wants to wash dishes? Not many people, but you will be surprised at how focusing on washing one dish can actually make you feel less anxious. Who knows, you may like it so much that this chore could become key to reducing your anxiety. To practice being mindful, you are going to practice washing one dish without thinking about anything else but washing the dish. Try it while you are home alone or tell the people you live with that you need ten minutes of quiet time while you wash the dish. Make sure any radios, TVs, or phones that you can hear are shut off—OFF, not on silent or vibrate. If any thoughts run through your head that are not related to washing the dish, just let them float away like clouds. Don't get mad at yourself for any other thoughts that enter your mind; just dismiss them and focus on what you are doing. Now, turn on the water and focus on how it runs over your hands, onto the plate, and into the sink. Be conscious of how the water feels on your hands: Is it warm? Hot? Put soap on the plate or dishcloth and notice how it comes out of the bottle. Does it smell good? Focus on the plate and how you feel while you are cleaning it. Doesn't it feel good to move a little? Do you need to scrub harder to get the plate as clean as it can be? When the plate is clean, rinse it and shut the water off. Dry the plate and notice how clean it looks. How do your hands feel? Can you still smell the soap?

Did any thoughts run through your head while you were cleaning the plate? Did you let them go? Was this a tough thing for you to do? It is really tough for most people! Do you feel relaxed now? How was it to have no stimulation and to focus on something that seems so simple? This is mindfulness!

If you can practice mindfulness in everything that you do, that would be fabulous. In all honesty, it's not easy in our world. So try to practice it once a day on something small, like washing your hair, peeling an orange, kneading bread, or petting your dog. As you get used to doing it, try it with other tasks. Whenever you are feeling anxious because too many things are running through your head, slow down and pick one task on which to focus. This should help reduce anxiety. Remember, during your mindfulness practice, try to notice how each sense was affected. Did you notice a smell, a taste, a feeling, a sight, or a noise? Maybe you never realized how good it feels to wash your hair until you really focus on rubbing shampoo into your head. Slowing down can definitely make some things that seem so insignificant seem relaxing and nurturing.

# Chapter 22

## Don't Forget to Breathe

Your body normally wouldn't let you forget to breathe. When anxiety takes over, however, our breathing can get really funky and make us even more anxious. In fact, even when we aren't anxious, it is rare that we take complete breaths. To breathe and get the most out of your breath, it is helpful to have great posture. How many people do you see each day who aren't slouched in their seats at school? Not many, and adults in office chairs are just as bad! If you can learn how to breathe fully when you aren't anxious, you will get the most out of your breath and use your breath to help decrease and prevent anxiety.

Why is breathing so important? Breathing brings oxygen into our bodies and takes stale air out. Oxygen is key for our bodies and can make our brains work better. Ever get tired in school and start to yawn? Yawning provides a way for the body to get more oxygen when it is feeling deprived. If you have been slouching in your seat all day, your brain may not be getting all the oxygen it needs because your breathing is shallow. Try to yawn. Can you feel all the air that comes into your body and how deep it goes—as opposed to your regular breath? Have you ever noticed that you yawn when you are nervous? This doesn't happen to everyone, but it does happen to some people. This is probably happening because our breathing becomes shallower when we get nervous. Yawning can remind the body to take deeper breaths. The following exercise will teach you how to breathe deeply and not only get more oxygen in, but also help you calm down your nervous system in times when you are feeling anxious.

**Out with the Old**

Breathe out all that stale energy and breathe in the good stuff. Learn how to take deep fulfilling breaths to help you relax. Have you ever watched a baby while he was sleeping? If so, you might have noticed that his belly goes up and down while he breathes. This is what you need to get back to—belly breathing! Right now, it is likely that you only breathe as deeply as your chest. You need to increase the breath you are taking in and make sure it gets as deep as it can.

Find a comfortable space where you will not be disturbed.

Make sure that your clothes are loose (for example, wear a comfy sweat-suit) and not digging into your body.

Lie on your back if that is comfortable or sit up comfortably. Remember, good posture is helpful in getting that good air in.

Put your hands gently on your belly.

Now take a deep breath. Did your shoulders go up? Did your belly go out? Did it feel weird? Notice how it was different from your usual breath. If your belly didn't move, you are going to need to breathe even more deeply.

This time, breathe in through your nose to a slow count of three (not 1, 2, 3, but 1 Mississippi, 2 Mississippi, 3 Mississippi).

Now breathe out to that same slow count.

Does this feel any different from the first deep breath you took? Hopefully, you are starting to move that breath in deeper.

Try it again, but this time, while you are breathing in, pretend that your body is like an empty glass that you need to fill up beginning with your belly. Get the oxygen down into your belly and let it fill your lungs. When you exhale, empty the glass completely.

Breathe in again. This time, as you fill your belly, imagine some of this nice new air traveling down to your toes. Now exhale and breathe out any stale air that has been stuck in those toes.

Practice this breathing for five to ten minutes a day and you will notice a difference in the way you breathe throughout your entire day. Practice will also make it easier for you to deep breathe at times when you are starting to feel anxious.

Before a test or presentation, even if you aren't that nervous, practice deep breathing because it will get more oxygen to your organs and it could help you concentrate on your task.

As you get to be a pro at this type of breathing, imagine that the breath that enters into your body is healthy, clean, colorful, or whatever you want it to be that is positive and relaxing. Imagine the breath that comes out is stale, old, negative, or anything you feel like getting out of your system.

Make this breathing your own and practice it daily as a way of beating anxiety before it can even get to you!

# Chapter 23

## Loosen Up

When anxiety is part of your everyday life, your muscles can become tense and your shoulders can start to creep up on you. If you can learn to recognize tense muscles and how to relax them, you will be able to get your body ready for relaxation just about anywhere. Have you ever gone out on a chilly day and looked at people around you? You might notice that when people brace themselves against cold weather, their shoulders creep up around their necks. You probably do it too, but you might not even notice because you are focused on the cold and staying warm, not on the position of your shoulders. It is important for your physical and mental health to develop some body awareness. When we worked on breathing, you learned to recognize that you don't breathe as deeply as you could and that when you're feeling anxious, your breath gets even shallower. The muscles in your body experience a similar phenomenon. When you are anxious, different parts of your body tense up. For some, it is their shoulders and neck; for others, it is their lower back. What happens over time, however, is that these muscles are so used to being tense, that you might not recognize that they are holding tension and therefore don't do anything about it because it feels normal. But tense muscles can lead to physical injuries and make your body stay in a physically anxious position when it really doesn't need to be.

Close your eyes for a minute. Do any parts of your body feel tense? Can you move them around a bit to relax them? Now look in the mirror. Do you see anything that looks tense? Shoulders? Jaw? Eyes? Do you have a feeling of tension but aren't really sure what part of your body is its source? You may recognize where you hold your tension and you may not. You may think it is one place when it is actually in a few! Try these activities to build some body awareness and learn how to decrease tension in your body.

## As Tense as You Can

Body part by body part, you will practice being as tense as possible and then as relaxed as possible. Practicing this activity can make you relax a body part on cue and really help with the physical feelings of anxiety. You can do this when you don't feel tense as a preventive measure, or you can do it when you are at your most anxious, ready to freak, angry, or in any keyed-up state of mind. It can help calm your body, distract you, and feel like a minimassage!

Find a place to sit that is comfortable and where you won't be disturbed by anyone.

You can close your eyes or keep them open, whichever you prefer. Sometimes closing your eyes can help you visualize the muscles you are working.

Make a tight, tight fist with both hands and squeeze for a count of five—remember to breathe as you feel how tight the muscles and tendons in your hands can be.

Release your fists and feel your fingers and hands relax. Do they tingle? Do you feel relief? Wiggle your fingers and hands. Rotate your wrists. Appreciate the difference between your tight, tight fists and your relaxed hands.

This is what tension and release feel like.

Shoulders are next. Bring your shoulders up as high as you can go and squeeze them up around your neck. Squeeze, squeeze, squeeze while you breathe for a count of five! Feel how tight they get and how restricted your neck feels with your shoulders up that high.

Drop those shoulders down. Breathe and just let your shoulders be as limp as possible. Move your head around and get some motion in that neck. Feel the difference. Do your shoulders feel even looser than before? Roll them out a bit. Breathe deeply as you feel them relax.

Now your face! You won't want anyone watching you for this one! Scrunch up your face, clench your jaw, squish your lips together, and squeeze those eyes shut. Hold for five seconds as you breathe despite all this squishing.

Release. Open your eyes wide, move your tongue and your jaw around. Raise your eyebrows up and down and wiggle them. Take a deep breath and notice any differences in your face. It's weird that your jaw can get so tight, your eyebrows can hold stress, and your eyes can actually open a lot wider than normal!

Now that you have the basic idea, try tensing and relaxing different body parts. You might even discover muscles you didn't know you had! One neat way of doing this is to start with the right foot, and travel all the way around your body, tensing and relaxing each individual muscle. Try it one night before bed and you may just sleep better.

Before a test, just doing this with your hands and shoulders might relax you enough to shake some of the pre-test jitters right out!

 ## Do You Yoga?

Learn some yoga poses and simple stretches to set your body into relaxation. These are just a handful of yoga poses that you can do to help relax or settle down at any time of the day. Yoga is an amazing tool to help calm anxiety, decrease depression, and improve sleep. The poses here are relaxing poses and nothing that is going to work up a sweat or have you balancing on your head. These are some simple poses and simple stretches you can do just about anywhere. There is no specific order; they were chosen just because they can make people feel relaxed!

Trying new things is fun; however, check with your doctor before trying something new like yoga. If you are pregnant or have any medical conditions, this is especially important. If anything feels uncomfortable at any time, stop doing it!

### Child's Pose

1. Kneel down and sit back on your heels.
2. Bend forward from your waist and stretch out your arms in front of you.
3. Stretch from your hips all the way to your fingers.
4. Feel your tummy resting on your thighs; your forehead is resting on the floor.
5. Either leave your arms in front of you stretched out, or place them alongside your body.
6. Breathe in and out through your nose. Stay as long as you are comfortable.

### Sit/Easy Position

1. Sit cross-legged with hands on knees.
2. Close your eyes and relax your shoulders.
3. Focus on your breath.

4. Take five to ten slow, deep breaths.

5. If you feel great, keep hanging out in this position and breathing!

## Corpse Pose/Savasana

This is a super way to relax!

1. Lie on your back with your eyes closed.
2. Let your feet flop out to the sides.
3. Turn your palms up to the ceiling and relax your hands.
4. Let your body sink into the floor.
5. Relax here for at least ten minutes.

## Simple Stretches

These stretches can all be done seated in a chair or in Sit Position from above.

**Neck:** Slowly drop your right ear to your right shoulder and feel a stretch through the left side of your neck. Slowly roll your head forward, bringing your chin to your chest and feel the stretch through the back of your neck. Now roll your left ear over to your left shoulder and feel the stretch through the right side of your neck. Slowly and carefully roll your head back, bringing your forehead toward the ceiling.

Repeat starting in the other direction.

**Shoulders:** Roll your shoulders forward, exaggerating the movement so that you are making big circles. Repeat three times. With the same exaggerated motion, roll your shoulders backward three times.

Now shrug your shoulders way up and release. Repeat three times.

**Upper back and chest:** Gently holding your left wrist with your right hand, extend both arms in front of you and stretch. Drop your head and round your back, really getting into that upper back. Now switch your hands so that you are holding your right wrist with your left hand and repeat.

If you are flexible enough, reach behind yourself and gently hold your left wrist with your right hand and roll your shoulders down and back as you stretch your arms behind you. Raise your chin slightly. Feel a stretch through the chest and shoulders. Switch hands and repeat.

## Yoga Classes

You are usually allowed one free class at most yoga studios, so taking a class is a great way to gain an introduction to yoga and to help you navigate any websites or books a bit more easily. Also, many yoga studios are willing to trade some work for free classes. If yoga seems to be the thing for you, talk to the manager of the yoga studio to see if you could trade some cleaning around the studio, or check-in work for free yoga!

Another great way to try yoga is on a DVD or on your computer. There are great DVDs at most public libraries (for free) and yoga lessons or podcasts on sites such as iTunes, also for free or close to it!

## Websites

**www.yogajournal.com/poses:** This is a great site that breaks down poses according to style of pose and even what ailments it can help (anxiety and insomnia are two). They give many of the names for the different poses in Sanskrit, but don't worry; you don't need to know another language to try them!

**www.yogasite.com/postures.html:** This site has sketched pictures of poses that are a little tough to transfer over to your body, but it includes really great descriptions of how different poses can be helpful.

**www.yogabasics.com/yoga-postures.html:** This site is cool because it has real people doing the poses and you can look up poses based on what you want to do—seated poses, standing poses, backbends, and others.

**www.abc-of-yoga.com/yogapractice/postures.asp:** My favorite of the bunch, this site is really easy to navigate and breaks yoga poses down into warm up, standing, seated, etc. In the yoga warm up area, they even help you warm up the muscles around your eyes.

**www.mayoclinic.com/health/stretching/SM00043:** This website has slideshows on how to stretch major muscle groups, how to stretch in your office, and more. It is filled with great information.

# Chapter 24

## World Traveler

Learn how to visualize yourself in a peaceful place like a beach or any other favorite place without anyone knowing. Being able to transport yourself to a peaceful, happy place prior to a big test or other stressful situation can relieve a lot of anxiety. Remember Chapter 20, when we found different objects that appeal to our senses? We will be doing something similar, but this time, instead of using tangible items, we will be using our imaginations to visualize a peaceful place, with relaxing sensations, pleasant smells, and positive energy. At first, you might need to take a look at the items you came up with in Chapter 20 to help inspire you. Maybe a picture of a beach will help you imagine you are there, or the smell of a lilac candle will help you visualize a peaceful image. Once you start practicing visualization, however, it will become easier and easier for you to do it without any tangible items. All you will need is your imagination. In fact, you probably do it already and don't even notice. Do you ever daydream about being out at the beach or somewhere other than where you are? Do you ever fantasize about what might happen in the future? That is basically visualization. So keep daydreaming—just try not to do it in class because the teacher might call on you!

Guided imagery is a type of visualization that can mentally lead you to a peaceful place. You can find examples of guided imagery on CDs or places like iTunes. The narrator usually has a pleasant and calm voice, and will ask you to get into a comfortable position and then take you through a journey to a beach, meadow, or other relaxing place. The narrator will speak about your breath, relaxing your body, the sounds, smells, and sights particular to the place you have gone to on your journey. As crazy as it sounds, it can be incredibly relaxing and it can release you from your stress and anxiety by changing the scenery in your mind. The activity that follows includes a guided imagery you can read to yourself, read into a recordable device to play back, or have someone read to you. It is a little tough to read to yourself while trying to visualize, but it can be done. If you read it enough, the idea of the journey will stick with you and you will be able to talk yourself through a guided imagery without even reading it. You can talk to yourself in your head; you don't have to talk out loud. The second guided imagery is more for fun, and will hopefully help you laugh and relax.

##  I Can Do That with My Eyes Closed

Practice this scripted visualization to help you come up with your own happy place to find yourself on stressful days.

Find a space that is comfortable and private where you can read this and just zone out. Make sure you are in comfy clothes and that you are nice and warm.

Take a deep breath, fill up your belly, and now exhale, releasing all the stale air that has been sitting in your belly all day. Try it again; this time sigh as you exhale.

Picture yourself on a beautiful beach. The water is a clear blue; the sand is soft underneath you. The only sounds you can hear are the gentle waves rolling into the sand and the occasional breeze rustling past. Breathe in the ocean air; it is fresh with a scent of salt and warmth. Let the air fill your lungs and reach all the way down to your toes. As you exhale, imagine all the air from your day leaving your body and clearing it out for more fresh salt air to enter. Take another deep breath in, filling your lungs and your body with peace. Listen as the water continues to gently hit the shore. Exhale any left-over stress from your day. Let the waves carry your stress out to sea.

As you inhale again, a warm breeze flows over your body, giving it a gentle massage. As it flows past, it takes with it any aches or pains, and leaves your body feeling light. Exhale any pain you have felt during the day and let the breeze surround you.

Inhale and notice how the sun is warming your toes and fingers. Exhale any cold, leaving room only for warmth. Let the warmth from your fingers and toes spread throughout your body and imagine the warmth is filling you with light. As you inhale, inhale the sweet salty smell, the healing power of the breeze and the warmth of the sun. As you exhale, let any stress, anxiety, and pain escape from your body. Imagine the stress being carried out to sea by the waves. Your anxiety and pain are carried away by the breeze. You are left only with the relaxation of the beach. Breathe slowly, enjoying your light body, no longer burdened by anxiety. Breathe slowly. You are in a peaceful place.

Breathe for as long as you would like to stay at the beach.

When you are feeling relaxed and ready, let the breeze pick up a bit and wiggle your fingers and toes. The breeze is still healing but it is also invigorating, bringing energy to your fingers and toes. Let the energy sparkle around you and take it in. Stretch your toes down and out. Reach your arms up over your head and stretch, making your body as long as it can be while inhaling the energy the breeze has given you. Exhale and relax. Slowly roll to your side and sit up if you are lying down. Deeply inhale and exhale. Take note of the relaxation within your body. Slowly open your eyes, or blink for a moment to bring yourself back to the here and now. All of your stressful energy is still out at sea, and the warm, healing energy is within you, ready to guide you through a peaceful day.

After a relaxation like this, you might feel tired or energized. No matter how you feel, be gentle with yourself and tune into what your body wants—perhaps a nap? A few stretches? Or is it invigorated and ready for a test or a workout? Listen to your body and remember you can go back to the beach at any time.

## Funny Relaxation

Have fun creating your own relaxation with a friend. Think Mad Libs meets Relaxation! Ask one of your friends to fill in the blanks. Don't tell her what the sentence is; just read the italics that indicate what type of word she needs to give you. Once it is all filled out, read it to her and help her through this hopefully relaxing and potentially hilarious visualization! Make a few copies and have someone ask you to fill in the words!

Imagine you are at _____. The weather is _____ and
*(favorite spot to relax)*                                        *(peaceful adjective)*

_____. It is quiet except for the sound of _____, which lulls you
*(peaceful adjective)*                                     *(sound)*

into a state of relaxation. There is a slight breeze that carries with it the scent of

_____. This scent brings you to a deeper state of relaxation and comforts
*(favorite scent)*

you, taking any stress away. As you inhale, imagine your breath filling your

body with the color _____, bringing peace and relaxation to
*(favorite color)*

your muscles, bones, and organs. Exhale slowly; imagine the air you breathe

out is _____, taking any negative energy out of your body—
*(least favorite color)*

leaving room only for positive energy. As you continue to breathe and feel

relaxed, imagine your _____ becoming heavy and let all the stress
*(body part)*

of the day leave your body. Breathe deeply, filling your body with _____
*(positive adjective)*

energy and letting out any _____ energy. Appreciate your body
*(negative adjective)*

for all that it does and relax for _____ cycles of breath Slowly wiggle
*(number)*

your _____ and start to wake your body up little by little.
*(body part)*

Breathe energy into all your body parts and take one final deep breath. Smile and slowly open your eyes. Your body is full of energy and life to carry you through your day.

Now that you are finished filling in the words, get comfy, either sitting or lying down, and get ready to relax!

# Chapter 25

## Move Your Booty

It is amazing how much better even a little movement can make you feel. You don't have to run a marathon, but a simple walk around the block can get some of that nervous energy out. This is a great way to prevent anxiety, too, and can be worked into your daily routine to help prevent stress. All it takes is a few minutes here and there to get the blood pumping in your body and to coax out those happy endorphins.

If you have never exercised before or if you think exercise is absolutely the most horrific thing in the universe, think of fun ways that you already move your body. Do you ever dance in your bedroom to your favorite song? Could you tolerate five minutes of jumping jacks? A quick sprint down the street? Think of something you would be willing to try and try it. Was there even a millisecond when your body felt happy or invigorated? Most likely there was. Exercise is absolutely amazing for your mind and body health. In order to make it work for you, find an exercise or a few exercises that you enjoy enough to do on at least a weekly basis.

Why is exercise so helpful, and why is it especially helpful for people with anxiety? There is no one answer, but according to the Mayo Clinic's website (www.mayoclinic.com/health/depression-and-exercise/MH00043), some research indicates that "exercise raises the levels of certain mood-enhancing neurotransmitters in the brain. Exercise may also boost feel-good endorphins, release muscle tension, help you sleep better, and reduce levels of the stress hormone cortisol. It also increases body temperature, which may have calming effects. All of these changes in your mind and body can improve such symptoms as sadness, anxiety, irritability, stress, fatigue, anger, self-doubt and hopelessness." Exercising is also described as providing an opportunity to boost self-confidence. Because you are doing something good for your body, exercise can help distract you from whatever is creating your stress. It is a way of dealing with anxiety that is a lot healthier than biting your nails or freaking out. A bonus benefit is that exercising can be pretty darn empowering. If you feel physically stronger, you will feel mentally stronger. If you used to worry that you didn't have the strength to protect yourself and, once you started exercising, you saw evidence of a biceps muscle, you might start to feel a little bit like a tough chick and a little less like a weakling. Let's find some activities that might be just what you need.

 ### Just Dance, Jump, or Run

Here is a list of activities with exercise routine suggestions—find your favorite way to move that body.

**Dancing:** You don't need to take a class or even be good at it. Shaking your hair out, moving your shoulders, and kicking your legs might be how you dance and that is just fine. Find two or three songs that you enjoy and that make you feel like moving, and put them together in a little mix. Now, play them in the privacy of your room and boogie down! Try this three times a week and see how it works for you. Is it working really well? Think about doing it more often! Would you like to try different styles of dance? Look up classes at your local gym or YMCA and see if they offer any fun classes like Zumba, country line dancing, hip-hop, and so on. Remember, this is for stress relief—not to become the best dancer in the world. Keep it fun!

**Walking:** Put one foot in front of the other. Literally. When you get mad, take a breather and walk around the block. After school, walk around the block. If doing your math is starting to make you panic, put down your books and walk around the block. Walk when you are stressed and walk when you are fine. Try walking for ten minutes three times a week. If you like how you feel, add ten minutes to the first ten minutes, or do another ten minutes later in the day. Try to build up to thirty minutes most days of the week. Remember, your walks don't have to be all in one chunk; you can break them up.

**Running:** Similar to walking, running is putting one foot in front of the other, except that it can be a little harder on your body. Start off slowly if you are not an experienced runner. Even jogging one minute and walking seven and jogging another minute and walking another seven can help ease your body into running. You might find that running fast for a short time makes you feel fabulous, while running slowly does nothing for you. On the other hand, running slowly might help you zone out and listen to a bunch of songs while you run. Find the running style that works best for you.

**Push-ups, sit-ups, jumping jacks:** These are great because, rain or shine, you can probably get away with doing them in your house. If you live on the second or third floor, you might have to do jumping jacks outside, but push-ups and sit-ups are nice and quiet! To start these, go for five or ten. Then build on that success. If you are feeling totally freaked, do jumping jacks until you start to feel giddy or less stressed. If you are angry, do push-ups and let that anger give you strength.

Other exercises that can be great include team sports through school or a city league, exercise classes like spinning or aerobics that you can take at a gym, fitness games you can play on your Wii or other game systems, DVDs you can find at the library, or supercool downloads you can find on iTunes. You can try just about anything! If you can afford it, meeting with a trainer at a gym is a great way to get an introduction to exercise and to make the gym a lot less overwhelming. Some gyms offer a free session or sessions with membership, and others offer free group instruction that introduces members to the equipment. One amazingly relaxing exercise that works your whole body is swimming. If you have access to a body of water, swimming is truly an amazing way of achieving calmness and getting a great workout. If you don't know how to swim, or are a bit uneasy in the water, just floating in the shallow water with a flotation belt can be helpful. There is something about feeling physically weightless that may actually make your mental weight seem a little lighter.

Before starting any exercise program, make sure that you check with your doctor that your body is ready to get a move-on.

Here are some great exercise websites:

**www.bam.gov/sub_physicalactivity/index.html:** This is the Centers for Disease Control and Prevention's website that talks about physical activity; it has some cool resources like activity cards, challenges, and general information.

**www.fitnessonline.com:** This website has a bunch of articles from popular fitness magazines that can be inspiring and often have some pretty cool workouts on them.

**kidshealth.org/teen/your_body/take_care/exercise_wise.html:** Yes, the name of the website is KidsHealth; however, there is a whole teen section on exercise, how much is enough, and the benefits of keeping your body healthy.

**www.itunes.com:** There are tons of cool podcasts here (some are free) that talk you through a yoga session, running route, or even a weight-lifting routine.

# Chapter 26

## Go to Bed!

Staying up till all hours of the night can make you a little crazy, and it will definitely add to your anxiety. Not sleeping makes you more agitated, irritable, forgetful, sensitive, prone to weight gain and clumsiness, slows your reaction time, and throws off your sleep schedule for nights to come. The funny thing about sleep is that you might not feel pooped the day after staying up all night or too late, but the day after that it will catch up with you. Making up for lost time with sleep isn't as helpful as getting what you need on a daily basis. Teenagers need about nine hours of sleep a night. That is more than most adults need, and it's almost impossible to get if you are a teenager who has to be at school by 7 or 8 a.m. Obviously, if you have to be there by say, 7:30, you need to get up, get ready, and get there. Let's say this takes you an hour and a half. That means you are getting up at 6! So, in order to get nine hours of sleep, you will need to go to bed by 9 p.m. and fall asleep right away. Does this sound like you or any of your friends? Probably not. Nevertheless, it is important to try really hard to get a solid amount of sleep.

Unfortunately for teenagers, your schedule works against you and it is *not your fault*. School starts way too early for your brain. The proof is in recent scientific research: teens' brains are set to go to bed later and to wake up later. If we put this research to good use and made school start later, we would probably have much happier, healthier, and brighter students! The National Sleep Foundation's website (www.sleepfoundation.org/site/c.huIXKjM0IxF/b.2419127/k.94D5/Teens_and_Sleep.htm) states that "biological sleep patterns shift toward later times for both sleeping and waking during adolescence—meaning it is natural to not be able to fall asleep before 11:00 pm."

So, as much as you may need that extra sleep, your brain might not want to cooperate with your school, work, sport, and "whatever else" schedules. With biology and scheduling working against you, what *can* you do to improve your sleep? You can improve what is known as sleep hygiene. Just like learning how to brush your teeth more thoroughly, use deodorant, and change your underwear, you can learn some tricks that will improve your quality, if not your quantity, of sleep.

## Sleep Tight

Chart your sleep habits for one to three days and find out what you can do to improve them. Little things such as eating too close to bedtime and going to bed at random times can be worked with and eventually help improve your sleep quality. Try to chart one weekend day (when you are likely to stay up later) like a Friday or Saturday and two weekdays. If you only do this for one day, pick an average weekday.

### Day 1

#### CAFFEINE:

1a. How many caffeinated beverages did you drink today (coffee, tea, soda, energy drinks, etc.)?

_____

1b. What time was your last caffeinated beverage?

_____

#### CHECK OUT WHERE YOU SLEEP:

2. Is it peaceful? Noisy? Comfortable? Too bright? Are your schoolbooks in bed with you? Is your laundry half folded and strewn across your bed? Are you sleeping in your day clothes? Write down anything that might get in the way of your sleep:

_____

RITUALS

3. For the hour before you tucked yourself into bed, did you:

- Eat
- Drink
- Watch TV
- Text
- Use computer
- Do homework
- Exercise
- Have a stress-ful conversation/interaction with someone
- Worry

- Gently stretch
- Practice breathing
- Read something mindless
- Meditate
- Prepare book bag
- Listen to soothing music
- Brush teeth
- Change into sleep clothes

Circle ALL that you did.

TIMING

4a. What time did you go to bed?

_____

4b. What time did you get up the following morning?

_____

Now that we have all these answers, let's take a look at improving your sleep hygiene.

**Caffeine:** Caffeine is a major culprit in the lives of all of us, but it does taste good and can be helpful at times. Can you cut down on the amount of caffeine you drink? If you drink three cups of coffee a day, can you cut down to half caffeine half decaf? If you live on energy drinks, can you swap one for water? Slowly cut down your caffeine intake to between none and one cup a day (remember a cup is eight ounces, not a fountain soda cup that is sixty-four ounces). Beware of cutting out caffeine cold turkey; it can cause headaches and make you ultracranky.

Caffeine is a drug and affects different bodies differently. For some, having a cup of caffeinated tea right before bed is no big deal, but for others, having a sip of caffeine after noon can disrupt their sleep. Try to cut out all caffeine after noon or 1 p.m. Again, do this slowly. If your last cup of caffeine is usually at 4 p.m., try to bump it back to 3 p.m. Continue making it earlier until your sleep improves.

**Where you sleep:** Oh boy! Do you have a peaceful bedroom? Or even a peaceful bed? So many teens do everything in their bed—from eating to texting to homework to sleeping. One of the best things to do to create a peaceful sleep space is to only allow yourself to sleep or relax on your bed. Everything else should happen elsewhere, even if that means the floor next to your bed or a chair next to your bed. Try and make your bed a mecca of sleep—not a multitasking piece of furniture. Your body deserves a calm place to sleep. If it has to share space with your books, laundry, cereal, and stress, it is not going to be a restful space.

How is your room set up for sleep? Is there a bright light that comes through a window? Is your alarm clock too bright? If so, find a way to cover the light with a curtain or even a towel.

Do you live on a busy street or in a busy area? Are sirens screaming by all night long? Invest in a pair of earplugs from a pharmacy and cut out any nonsoothing noise.

Try and make your bedroom as peaceful as you can. Chances are a lot goes on in your bedroom since it is probably one of the few places you can get any privacy, so you may just need to focus on your bed as a calm space and leave your bedroom a little hectic. If possible, however, cover anything stressful prior to bed. Are you going to stare at schoolbooks and worry all night about upcoming exams? Then move them from your view—cover them, put them in the hallway, whatever, but don't let them invade your sleep space!

**Rituals:** Your goal for rituals is to create a ritual or two that helps you prepare for bed—something soothing that helps set the stage for a good night's sleep. Taking part in a bedtime ritual can signal to your body that it is time to wind down, relax, and get ready to snooze. Many of us have rituals that we don't even realize we have, and some of them, instead of helping us sleep, can actually make it harder to sleep. Let's go over what you circled.

Anything you circled in the first column—stop doing it at least one hour before bed. Eating and drinking can wake you up. Drinking certain things like relaxing teas or warm water might be helpful, but if you find you are waking up in the middle of the night to pee a lot, consider drinking anything like this at least one hour before bedtime.

Watching television, texting, and using the computer can all stimulate your brain. The screens on televisions and computers can cause your brain to wake up, so put those to rest an hour before bedtime. *Shut your phone off!* If it rings, vibrates, or makes some other weird noise, it is only going to disrupt your efforts to settle into sleepy time mode.

Doing homework might be a necessity right up until the final hour, but if possible, take some time off between homework and bed. Doing anything stressful right before tucking in isn't going to help you sleep. Who wants to dream about algebra and the anatomy of the worm?

Exercise, while strongly encouraged to help with sleep and anxiety, can be so invigorating that it will wake your body up if you do it too close to bedtime. Try to make time for exercise in the afternoon so that your body can relax as bedtime nears.

Stressful interactions before bedtime can cause worry. Unfortunately, you can't control other people, so completely controlling stress caused by others is nearly impossible to do. What you can control, however, is when you shut your phone off for the night, or which friends you cut off earlier than others. If your best friend is a total drama queen, try keeping your conversations with her to a minimum at night. Is there a friend you aren't getting along with very well? Talk to her during the day. Leave nighttime chats for light and happy conversations.

Worrying is another tough thing to control. For many people, as soon as they close their eyes, all the worries of the day and worries for tomorrow race through their minds, keeping their brain on overdrive. One helpful way to combat this is to keep a notebook next to your bed where you can write down your worries as they try to butt into your sleep. Write them down and agree to worry about them tomorrow. For now, you need to sleep, so pluck the worrying out of your brain and put it in the notebook.

What about all the words you circled in the second column? YIPPEEE!!! These are healthy, sleep-enhancing rituals that you can continue doing or start doing if you have never done them before! Use the healthy stretches to relax your body from Chapter 23, use breathing techniques you learned in Chapter 22, or any of the relaxation techniques you have learned that you find helpful. You don't have to do them for the full hour prior to bed; even five to ten minutes of relaxation prior to bed can really calm your mind and body and prepare you to sleep.

If none of the relaxation techniques have tickled your fancy up until now, try something simple to help get your body into sleep mode. Flipping through a mindless magazine, brushing your teeth, prepping your clothes and book bag for the next day, or even changing into your comfy sleep clothes might be enough to say to your body and mind, "Okay, it's time to settle down and get ready for a great night of sleep!"

**Timing:** This is a big one and a tough one. If you go to bed at totally different times every night, you are making your system more haywire than it already is. Try as best you can to go to bed at around the same time every night. Is it impossible over the weekend? Fine. Work on the weekdays. If you go to bed at 9 some nights and at 11 other nights, find a happy medium like 10 and make that your goal every night. The closer you can keep the times at which you go to bed, the easier it will be for your body to find a rhythm.

What time you need to get up is also important because it tells you how many hours you are sleeping, and whether you are waking up at similar times every morning. If you are sleeping less than seven hours, you need to make some serious changes. Go to bed thirty minutes earlier until you are at least aiming for eight hours of sleep. Is eight enough? No, but it is better than five. Similar to going to bed at more or less the same time every night, waking up at a similar time will also help your body find a rhythm in your sleep patterns. So, try to wake up close to the same time every morning.

That, in a nutshell, is sleep hygiene. There is a lot that goes along with it, and to be honest, trying to perfect it is not the goal. Trying to improve it is. Your body and brain really need sleep. As a teenager, both your body and brain are incredibly busy. Let them rest and you will gain HUGE benefits. Maybe the only change you will make after reading this chapter is to start listening to soothing music prior to bed. That is fine. You are at least recognizing that sleep is important and making an effort to improve yours.

If sleep is a horrible issue for you, talk about it with your primary care physician. Sleeping is as important as eating. Without it, your body just won't work the way it needs to, so see your doctor if sleep is difficult for you.

# Chapter 27

## Did You Have Your Vegetables Today?

The food that you choose can have an impact on your anxiety. If you survive on fast food, soda, coffee, and sugar, you can bet that you are not going to feel your best. Making better food choices can improve concentration and reduce anxiety. Understanding healthy food choices, the dangers of certain foods, and the benefits of getting the right nutrition can make your overall health improve in many ways.

Let's start with the good stuff. Thankfully, fast-food restaurants and convenience stores are making healthy food choices much easier to find. There was a time when finding a salad meant making one or going to a nice restaurant. Now you can find salads, yogurt, fruits, and more just about anywhere. Fruits and vegetables are superimportant. They are filled with things like antioxidants, fiber, and vitamins. Getting enough fruits and veggies in your diet can improve your skin, digestive health, and even boost brainpower! Apples, blueberries, kiwis, bananas, green beans, broccoli, and cauliflower are great fruits and vegetables. Challenge yourself to try one new fruit or veggie each week and see how many new ones you can discover!

Lean protein is another important food group that should be included in your diet every day. Protein is a building block in our bodies and helps our muscles grow, our minds focus, and our bodies recover from any intense exercise. Protein also can make you stay full longer and keep you from crashing. Examples of lean protein include chicken breast, egg whites, soy protein (like tofu), and 99 percent fat-free ground turkey.

Carbohydrates can be tricky. We really need carbohydrates in our diets to help keep us filled with fiber, awake, and getting key nutrients; however, there are different kinds of carbohydrates and telling the difference between healthy ones and not so healthy ones can be kind of tough. The most nutrient-dense carbohydrates include foods like whole wheat bread, unsweetened oatmeal, brown rice, whole-wheat pastas, and grains like quinoa (don't knock it till you try it; it is actually quite delicious!). Less nutrient-dense carbohydrates include most white or very processed foods like many cookies and crackers, white pasta, and white rice. These can make some people feel sluggish, get hungry again soon after eating, and crash. This doesn't mean these foods are "bad." It just means that substituting some more nutrient-dense ones here and there can really benefit your diet by adding fiber, whole grains, and other vitamins that aren't always available in the more processed carbohydrates.

Dairy doesn't always get a great rap. Many foods that are considered dairy products do contain high amounts of fat and sugar, and you do have to be a little careful when loading up on them. Milk is great source of dairy, but whole milk has a lot of fat so be careful and go for something like 2 percent, 1 percent, or even skim, which will give you the nutritional benefits without the saturated fat. Yogurt is another dairy product that comes in a variety of fat contents, but also comes with different levels of sugar. Some sweetened yogurts have the same amount of sugar as a candy bar! Try to stick to plain yogurt and add your own fruit, or go for yogurt that has real fruit added, not sugar! Dairy contains calcium that is good for your growing bones.

Fat is not all bad. Your body needs fat to work properly, and healthy fats like unsaturated fats can help many processes in your body work well and even keep your skin looking fabulous. Unfortunately, your favorite candy bar probably doesn't have the right kind of fat, but there are plenty of foods that do. Nuts, avocados (guacamole—yum!), nut butters, olive oil, and salmon are all foods that contain healthy fats to add to your diet.

Water is absolutely necessary. We need water to live and being properly hydrated can make you less hungry and more awake, help your skin, help get anxiety out of your system, and more! Since water can flush your body out, it can help your body get rid of the chemicals your body produces when you feel anxious. As your body gets rid of these chemicals, your anxiety can decrease and you can feel more relaxed. If you hate the taste of water, try adding a little lemon or orange juice for some flavor. If that is still totally gross to you, try adding some 100 percent juice to your water. This will increase the calories and sugar, but it might help you get the fluid into your body that you need. If you exercise a lot, be sure to drink water to replenish!

Some of the foods that can negatively affect your health and your anxiety level include processed foods, sugary foods, caffeine, and fatty foods.

Caffeine is perhaps the most crucial in terms of anxiety. It is found in coffee, tea, chocolate, soda, and those energy drinks everyone seems to be drinking. Caffeine can be beneficial in some instances. Some research has found that certain amounts of caffeine can enhance performance; however, if you have too much, it can make you jittery (as if you don't jitter enough when anxious!), irritable, unable to sleep, make your heart pound, and cause your body to crash after a while. Many people tolerate caffeine with no problem, while others seem very affected by it. If you love caffeine and the thought of giving it up is anxiety provoking, then just try to cut it down a bit. Make your morning coffee the only caffeinated one. If you have trouble sleeping, cut out caffeine after school. If jitters are an issue, don't overdo caffeine on a day that you are already anxious; drink water instead. Take note of how caffeine affects you and keep in mind that your best friend may be able to drink energy drinks until 11 p.m. and sleep like a baby, but your body may need to put caffeine to rest at 11 a.m. in order to sleep soundly at 11 p.m.

As far as sugary foods, processed foods, and fatty foods go, they just aren't that great for you. It doesn't mean you have to banish them from your diet forever, but keep an eye on your intake of these foods. Fatty foods can make some people feel sluggish, sugary foods can make some people bounce off the wall and then crash, and some people find that processed foods cloud their thinking and make them not feel so hot. It is one of those trial-and-error issues for many of us, but eating food that makes you feel healthy, strong, nourished, and alert is a good way to gauge foods that should be keepers in your daily diet!

If you would really like to learn about the food that you are putting into your body and to find out if these foods are good choices, the website www .mypyramidtracker.gov has many cool tools and much helpful information. It is a fun and interactive website with tips for teens, athletes, kids, and more. There are some books out there with good advice and tips, but for the best advice, ask your doctor for a referral to a nutritionist if you really want to work on healthy eating. Following a diet plan designed for you and your growing body and developing brain is really important. Diets on the Internet and in magazines might be great for a movie star playing the next bionic woman, but they probably won't give you the nutrients you need to be your healthiest. Take advice from health professionals, not television advertisements or magazines.

## My Own Menu

By charting your food intake and how you feel before and after eating certain foods, you can come up with your own optimal menu from which to choose healthy foods. For the next three days, keep track of the foods you eat, the time you eat them, and your mood, energy, and hunger levels before and after you eat them. Based on this information, you can get a better idea of what foods you might want in your daily diet and foods you might want to eat only occasionally or not at all. Any food that leaves you feeling tired, sluggish, cranky, angry, or overexcited is a food to consider eating sparingly. Foods that make you feel full, but not too full, even-keeled, and alert are keepers. The importance of keeping track of times that you eat is that some foods might make you feel really full right afterward, but then you find yourself hungry again an hour later. These foods might not have enough staying power for you, so you might want to trade them in for more nutrient-dense foods. Hunger level is important to look at because you might find that you are eating every day at 3 p.m., but that you aren't really that hungry. Alternatively, you might find that you are starving by 3 p.m. and letting yourself get too hungry before eating. What does mood have to do with it? Do you find that you eat when you are anxious? Do you skip meals when you are anxious? What about boredom? Can you plow through a bag of chips because you are bored, but actually not hungry at all? Try and feed your hunger—not your mood! All of these things will help you pick and choose foods that make you feel your healthiest. Once you have found these foods, make them staples in your diet. Whether or not these foods impact your anxiety directly is important; however, eating foods that make you feel healthy in general can indirectly impact your anxiety since you are taking care of your body and nourishing your mind, body, and soul.

Here is a note of advice. You have heard it before, but breakfast really is important. Eating breakfast—even if you can only eat some toast—will help get your body going in the morning. If you aren't eating breakfast, start!

## Food, Mood, and Energy Tracker

| Time | Pre-Hunger Level (Not at all, Kind of, Starving) | Pre-Hunger Mood (Low, Good, High) | Pre-Hunger Energy | Food | Post-Hunger Level (Not at all, Kind of, Starving) | Post-Hunger Mood (Low, Good, High) | Post-Hunger Energy |
|---|---|---|---|---|---|---|---|
| | | | | | | | |
| | | | | | | | |
| | | | | | | | |
| | | | | | | | |
| | | | | | | | |
| | | | | | | | |

Now look back at what you wrote. Did chips make you crash twenty minutes later? Did the apple you had after school keep you satisfied and improve your mood? Stick to the foods that gave you energy, boosted your mood, and made you feel good!

# Chapter 28

## Our Friendship Knows No Bounds

But it should. In this chapter, learn how to set boundaries for yourself. If you do everything for everyone, you might be a "great friend," but who's taking care of *you*? You won't be able to sustain taking care of others if you don't take care of yourself. Learning to set boundaries now will work wonders for you in the future. Ever have a day where curling up on the couch at home and watching cheesy movies sounds perfect? Then a friend calls and tells you she really needs you right now; she just found out another friend is bad-mouthing her. Could you please come over? Some days, you might feel happy to run right over. On other days, you might regret answering the phone, groan, go over to her house, and feel annoyed the whole time you are with her because you really want to be curled up on your couch—not with her and her whining. Does this mean you are a bad friend? No, but it *does* mean you need to pay more attention to yourself and your needs and to address those needs first. Then, when your friend needs you, you can listen to her without wishing she would shut her trap.

If your body and mind are saying, hey, let's have a relaxing day at home away from all the drama, where we don't have to worry about anything but being comfy and finding the cheesiest movie possible, LISTEN. You need a break. Everyone does. As great as your social life might be, socializing can be rather exhausting. People have different tolerances for it. Some people can go out two nights a week and then all weekend and not feel drained on Monday; others might be able to hang with the best of them on Friday and Saturday but need Sunday to rejuvenate and then the rest of the week to store energy for the coming weekend. These variations are normal. As different as our social tolerances are from one another, they also can differ for us at different points in our lives. Perhaps you are having a stressful month at school, or something is going on in your family that is making you feel emotionally exhausted. You might find that you are feeling as though you don't have much energy for social occasions. This may ebb and flow throughout your life. Keep tabs on how you are feeling. Is your social energy running low? Then stay home and let it build a bit. If you push it while it is low, you risk being a party pooper, a nonlistener, a friend who is totally irked by her friends, or compromising your relations in other ways. If you let your energy build up, you will have the energy to really be present for your friends when they need you. You can listen to them, laugh with them, and have a higher tolerance for any annoying behaviors.

Friends and family often put enormous pressure on you. Setting boundaries can feel like you are not being a great friend or relative. It might feel like this to them at first. If you were always the one they could call when they were upset, hearing you tell them you can't talk right now could be tough to swallow. If you explain, however, that you are socially or emotionally pooped and need some time for yourself, they will hopefully respect that and realize that when your social energy tank is full, you will be a much more attentive and fun friend.

 ### Gee, I Would Love to, But...

Learn how to say no without making friends feel neglected. Here are a few different scenarios you might face and some ideas on how to address them.

1. You made a commitment to someone already and are feeling pretty wiped out. Well, try your hardest to follow through since you have already committed, but keep in mind that the next time you make plans, put off solidifying them until you know you are feeling up to it. If you are truly running on empty, consider shortening the time you are going to spend with your friend, or changing plans to something more low key. Simply explain, "I am so happy we have plans to hang out, but I am wiped out after a superbusy week. Is it cool with you if we meet an hour later? I can take a quick nap to perk up so I am not totally lame and falling asleep on you as soon as we go out!"

   That way, you are letting your friend know that you still want to see her, even though you are tired. You also are letting her know that she is important enough to you that you want to be available to her and not snoozing while you're together.

2. You made plans for the weekend at the beginning of what looks to be a stressful week. Perhaps your friends decided to have a party on Friday night to celebrate the end of a stressful week. The party might even be a motivator to get through a tough week. In your experience, however, weeks like this are exhausting for you and you just don't know if you can party after all that stress. You could hold them off a bit: "You guys know what a zombie I am if I am stressed. Let me see how I feel on Friday. If I am not the walking dead, I will totally be there!"

   If you already know that you will be too pooped to party, let them know: "I love you guys and I wish I had your energy at the end of the week. Maybe we can do something on Saturday? I think I'm going to need Friday night to totally veg out and relax."

   Alternatively, you could try to change their plans to something more relaxing, but don't be offended if they still want to party: "Well, I really want to hang out with you guys, but I don't think I am up for a party. What if we give ourselves pedicures and have snacks early on Friday to celebrate? That way, your feet will look awesome for the party, and I can spend time with you, then go to bed!"

3. A friend who is having a tough time keeps calling and is starting to get on your nerves. You find yourself wanting to avoid her, but you also feel bad because you know she is hurting and needs a friend. This is a tough one, but it is hard to be compassionate when you feel like someone is draining the energy out of you. You can set a boundary with this friend in a couple of different ways. One way is to put a limit on how long you talk: "Hey, Lana, I can only talk for twenty minutes. How are you?" This puts a limit on how long she has to talk and could actually help her tell you only the important parts of what she needs to say. Another way is to schedule a time to talk to her later in the week, when you feel like you can be available to her: "Hey, Lana, I would love to talk, but I am feeling pretty tired right now. Why don't we make plans to talk on Wednesday and then I can give you my full attention?" If you generally enjoy talking to Lana but feel like she is droning on and on about the same thing, you could decide that you will only talk about that subject for a certain amount of time or not at all:

"I know your breakup with Randy has been awful, Lana, but to be honest, it is wicked annoying to hear about it all the time. I feel like my friend Lana has disappeared in this breakup! Let's make a deal to talk about anything BUT Randy!"

4. Perhaps you are dealing with people who just don't take a hint. This is for the person who, despite your kind attempts to set limits, continues to steal more of your time or make you feel guilty about not spending enough time with her: "Janet, I really want to stay friends, but sometimes I feel like you can't take no for an answer when I don't feel like talking or hanging out. I really need 'me time'—as silly as that may sound. Having you tell me that I'm not a good friend because I'm taking that time really makes me feel like you can't respect my needs. Maybe we should take a little breather from our friendship until we both feel a little less stressed." Point out to your friend that you would like to continue being her friend, but it will have to be on terms that suit you both. You have every right to have time to yourself, and you find that time to yourself allows you to be a better friend. If she can't respect that, she isn't respecting you enough and may not be able to be one of your friends for the time being.

5. Family. They get their own category. Unfortunately, telling your dad you need "me time" when he needs you to pick up your filthy room probably won't get you very far and may leave you with *a lot* of "me time" when he grounds you for talking back. Explaining your needs to your family—especially to adults who may need you to help out—can be tough. It may help to talk to them about your needs when there is no other conflict occurring. After dinner, when your parent or guardian has had his own "me time" could be the perfect time. "Hey, Dad, lately I've been pretty stressed. I think it might be helpful if I could have a little time to myself every day to regroup before starting my chores. I think that will help me do them better and with less grumbling." You aren't asking to get out of anything or to have your chores reduced, so it is likely that the adult in your life will respect that you need some time to yourself. If not, you might have to find a way to take time when he isn't around, or to get your chores done and then take time. If you aren't able to have any time to yourself and this becomes a big problem, talking to a counselor who can help you talk to your parent or guardian might be the way to go.

# Chapter 29

## Over and Over Again

For some people, mindless or mindful repetitive motion is extremely stress reducing. Think about how we soothe babies: we rock them. Find your own way to rock yourself to relaxation—kneading bread, petting a dog, or even rocking in a rocking chair. Little tricks like these are often the most powerful. There are two ways of practicing; one is mindlessly, just letting your mind wander while you practice your activity, and the other, mindfully, we addressed in Chapter 21. To practice any of these suggestions mindfully, you would be more focused on the action and paying attention to how your body feels as you practice. Either one can bring you to a state of relaxation; you just need to figure out which one works best for you! Sometimes, you might start a motion mindlessly, but as you repeat the motion, you become more mindful. Kneading dough is a great example; you might be totally spaced out while kneading and then notice your attention is brought to how the dough feels, how your hands feel while working the dough, the smell, how your muscles respond to the dough, and so on. It is pretty cool!

 **Knit, Bake, Paint—Which One Strikes Your Fancy?**

Here are some activities to try:

**Baking:** Find a recipe for bread that you must knead and see if the action of kneading is soothing. Look for recipes that you need to stir quite a bit—don't use beaters or a food processor. Use a spoon and see if that is an action that makes you feel a bit calmer.

**Crafts:** Pick up a hobby like knitting or crocheting in which there is a repetitive movement and rate your relaxation. Remember, you don't have to perfect this or even be any good at it. This is all about helping your mind and body find a calm state.

**Chores:** Does your neighbor need a room painted? Would you earn brownie points for ironing or vacuuming? The motion of painting a wall can be quite soothing—just try not to get too frustrated by corners or any areas that you need to paint around. Ironing and vacuuming are great ideas, too, because you accomplish housework while relaxing!

Give them all a try and see if any work for you. Get creative and come up with more options!

# Chapter 30

## Just Say Om

You may feel that meditation is a bit too weird for you. But do at least try just one exercise in this chapter; no one will even know. Meditation doesn't have to involve sitting with your legs crossed chanting "Om." It takes many different forms, all of which can be extremely helpful. In fact, some would argue that the activities from the preceding chapter, "Over and Over Again," are actually a moving form of meditation. Similar to repetitive motion, meditation can use repetition as well. For many, it is helpful to concentrate on a word, thought, sentence, wish, or idea to get into a state of meditation. In one's head, one might repeat a word over and over again as she clears her mind of any other thoughts or stressors. Repeating a word or phrase gives the mind something to focus on so that it is not distracted by who asked you or didn't ask you to the prom, why Sally didn't invite you to the mall, or how stressed you are about your upcoming English exam. This is the kind of meditation we are going to try.

## My Own Mantra

Create your own one- to two-word mantra that puts you in a positive space—or at least makes you smile for a second! First of all, what is it that you need? Do you need to gain clarity on a situation with a friend? Do you need more focus in class? Do you wish you had more patience with people? Do you need to calm down or relieve anxiety? Answer that question and find a word that sums it up (for example, clarity, focus, patience, or calmness). Do you have your word? Write it here:

_____

Now, is that one word enough? Could you repeat it to yourself to get in a zone where you are actually creating it, or do you need a couple of more words?

Try the word on its own and see how it feels. If you feel you need a couple of more words, try these out in front of your word to create a sentence:

I feel _____.

I am _____.

I have _____.

Better? Presenting your idea as something you already feel, are, or have, creates a positive energy around it. You feel calm, you are focused, and you have patience. Telling yourself that these words you hope to attain are already within you can help you believe that you truly are capable of becoming these words. A fun note about mantras is that you can have as many as you need! Maybe you need different mantras for different situations. Maybe you can attain focus but now would like to work on compassion. Whatever the case, your mantra is your mantra and no one can tell you it is wrong. It is personal and you don't need to share it with or explain it to anyone.

## Putting Your Mantra to Use

Now that you have your mantra, what do you do?

Find a quiet place where you won't be disturbed by people, technology, or any discomforts.

Get comfortable. Sit against a wall if that helps you feel supported, or sit with your legs crossed on your bed.

Find a point in your room that will not move and focus on it. It can be a picture of something that makes you feel calm, or just an old hole in the wall. As long as it won't move or distract you, it should do just fine.

Now start breathing deeply while keeping focused on the point you chose.

Inhale slowly, and as you exhale, say your mantra slowly to yourself.

Repeat this practice for at least five minutes.

As you continue to repeat your mantra, you may notice that you are not really seeing the point you focused on, but you are somewhat spaced out or focused internally. Go with it and enjoy your state of mind.

Try practicing for five minutes a day five days in one week. Take note of how you feel before, during, and after your practice. Are you more relaxed? Is your breathing deeper? Did you miss a day? How did that make you feel? Any differences on days you practiced compared to days you didn't? Did you find yourself sneaking in any extra mantras to help relax? Keep trying it. Try new mantras if one doesn't seem to work for you!

Once you practice enough, you will find that you can get yourself into a state of relaxation just about anywhere at any time.

# Chapter 31

## Practice Makes Perfect

It's true. The more you practice, the better you will become at whatever you are trying to learn. Will you be perfect at it? Not necessarily, but if you practice a lot, you are more likely to pull off what you are doing with greater ease and less stress. Think about athletes. They practice crazy amounts of time to get better at their sport. Have you ever seen athletes warming up, or prepping before a big game or event? Sometimes they don't have the space or equipment to actually practice their routine. If you watch figure skating, you may have seen a competitor, prior to taking the ice, with her eyes closed, going through motions of a routine in her head—no skates on, no jumps, and no spins. She may be using her arms a bit, maybe even listening to her performance music, or sitting quietly in a corner. This technique is called visualization; it is a little like daydreaming. The figure skater who visualizes her routine usually not only visualizes all the moves she has to do, she also visualizes completing the moves precisely, the roar of the crowd, the smile she will flash to the judges, and the wave she will give the audience as they stand and applaud her incredible performance. All of this goes on in her head to prepare for the real event. Many athletes practice visualization because it creates a "movie" of the performance they hope to achieve. Visualizing a successful performance also can help you perform well and boost your self-esteem.

Visualization doesn't have to be only for athletic events. You can use it for just about everything. Nervous about a job interview? Worried that you might sound like a blubbering idiot or not greet your interviewer correctly? Close your eyes and imagine walking into the interview with a pleasant smile and great confidence. You shake your interviewer's hand while you make eye contact. Now visualize yourself answering questions with ease—perhaps even laughing with the interviewer. At the end of the interview, you stand up, smile, shake hands, and walk out feeling great. Visualizing scenarios like this can be a way of creating your own private practice session. In cases like interviewing, it is helpful to have some real practice interviewing, but in between real practices, visualization is a great way to rehearse and build self-confidence.

If you are really stressed out about a particular event that is coming up, your attempts at positive visualization may be laced with negative tidbits here and there. If you are visualizing an upcoming presentation, your mind might play a trick on you; for example, in your head, you might drop your note cards. DON'T BE FRUSTRATED. If your visualization doesn't go perfectly, take it in stride. Pick up those note cards in your head and visualize how you would handle such an adverse event. This is actually a great way to rehearse a potential glitch in your performance. The more you visualize the event, the less you will probably find that those little demons sneak in and make your visualization less than perfect.

A great time to visualize an upcoming event is when you are getting ready to go to sleep. End the day with a positive visualization. Don't have anything coming up to visualize? Find something! Visualize waking up in a good mood and staying in a good mood throughout the day!

## The Big Day

Pick an upcoming event that you have some anxiety about and practice how the event might go in your head. Practice the best outcome and imagine that this is the outcome you will achieve. Imagine what you will be wearing that day, that you are calm, and that you are prepared. Picture yourself taking a deep breath, relaxing your body, and smiling because you know you are going to do well. Go through the event in your head, remembering that you are relaxed and prepared. You've got this, no problem! The outcome is just as you had hoped. Imagine yourself enjoying your success and smiling. Now take this visualization and make it happen!

# Chapter 32

## The Heat of the Moment

What happens if you are somewhere away from home and your anxiety starts to get the best of you? What if you have a panic attack, throw up, or faint? You would be smart to plan escape strategies prior to having to make one. Often, just knowing an escape is possible will relax you sufficiently so that you won't need one. Let's hope this won't happen. You can put all of the skills you have learned thus far into practice. Visualize something occurring prior to the actual event. Before entering, try some deep breathing. Scope out someone you know who makes you feel comfortable. Feeling anxious as you arrive at a place? Ground yourself. Remember, you are in control. If you feel as though these activities and others from previous chapters aren't enough and, in the heat of the moment, you start to feel panicky, make sure you are prepared to handle a quick escape!

### What to Do

If you are going to a new venue—a party at someone's house or a new after-school activity—get the lay of the land right away. Find out where the exits are. Does a certain door lead to the outside? Can you reenter? Maybe there is a door that leads to a hallway where you can take a quick break if you need one. Where are the bathrooms? Position yourself close to the bathroom area. Everyone has to pee, so running to the bathroom is perfectly acceptable. Are you someone who gets "dry mouth" in stressful situations? Find a water bubbler. You can always take a time-out. The cool thing about mapping out potential break spaces is that you will be well prepared in case you do get anxious; you also will keep yourself busy for a bit while you are figuring out where everything is located. If someone approaches and asks if you know where he or she can get some water or find the restroom, you will know! You might not wind up needing to use any of these things, but knowing where these areas are can alleviate anxiety.

## What to Say

Is the heat of anxiety creeping up your face? Is your body starting to feel shaky? Different scenarios will allow for different excuses. If you are in a large group setting and the attention is not on you, you can probably scoot out for a minute without telling anyone where you are headed. If someone does ask, you can chuckle and say, "Too much water!" No one is going to tell you that you can't go to the bathroom; if someone does, that is weird, so you should go anyway!

If you are in a conversation with someone and anxiety suddenly overwhelms you, say something like, "Excuse me, I need to step outside for just a moment." You don't need to explain yourself. Most people won't inquire further. Upon your return, a caring person might ask if you are okay. You can simply answer "yes," or shrug and say something like, "Well, if I faint, call my mom!"

If you are feeling as though you cannot possibly continue, one way of getting out easily is to make yourself cough and excuse yourself for some water. That way, your anxiety isn't at the forefront and you will appear to have a very good reason to jet out. Once you are at the water bubbler, take some deep breaths. See if you can relax before heading back in.

## What to Try

Make a checklist for your pocket or purse that has all of your favorite strategies written on it. Try them. If you find that you're still incredibly anxious, give yourself a time-out. Take a walk down the hall or around the building while you think of something spectacular you will do for yourself after the event is over. You might have to bribe yourself by promising yourself something special like a new baseball glove or handbag if you make it through the event. Give yourself something to look forward to and remind yourself that if you have made it this far, you can complete the event. This is just one event in your entire life; you are much more than this one event. This one moment does not define who you are or who you can be. It is simply something to get through and move past.

You can do it.

# Part IV

When You Need More

First of all, you should never feel like you have to fight the anxiety battle on your own. Talking to any safe adult in your life is a recommendation for when you first start to feel anxiety. There may come a time, however, when you still feel anxious despite trying every single exercise in this book or other books. When this happens, it is really important to enlist the help of others.

# Chapter 33

## Counseling

There are many different types of counseling and different types of counselors. In some areas, school counseling is available; in others, outpatient therapy is your only choice. Also, you might be more comfortable with group counseling or individual counseling. So let's take a look at all the different possibilities.

## Types of Counseling
### School Counseling

If you are currently in school, school counseling could be the perfect solution. Usually it takes place during the school day, and it is generally provided by a counselor who is employed by the school or has an agreement with the school that allows her to come in and provide counseling services. Think about the following issues in considering school counseling:

1. Can you handle talking about tough stuff in school? If your counselor sees you during third period and you have math fourth period, can you pull yourself together in time to get to math and then make it through the rest of the day? If not, you might be better off with an end-of-the-day appointment or even a counselor that you see outside of school.

2. Will you be embarrassed being taken out of class by the counselor? Chances are, if you are going to go to in-school counseling, other students will know. They might come up with their own ideas about why you are going to counseling. School counseling tends to be a bit less private just because of the setting.

3. What type of counselor will you see, a guidance counselor or school adjustment counselor who is employed by the school, or someone from an outside agency? This is good to know because the limits of confidentiality can differ. Sometimes school-employed counselors have to share more of your business with school administrators and teachers. Be sure to ask whomever you are considering working with what his policy is about talking to school administrators and teachers. If there are specific things you would like to keep confidential, make sure they can be kept confidential before talking about them.

4. Does this counselor have an office outside the school where you can see her after school hours or during school vacations? Is the counselor allowed to see patients from school outside school? If the person is a school employee, she might not have office hours during school vacations and summers, so you have to think about how a break in your counseling might affect your progress.

## Outpatient Counseling

Outpatient counseling includes counseling that takes place at a private practice, a mental health clinic, some hospitals, and primary care offices. This is a type of counseling in which you would meet with your counselor in an office setting. There are some things to keep in mind if you are considering outpatient counseling:

1. Is it easy to get to? If it is too far away, or you can't drive or don't have access to public transportation, getting to appointments could become a problem. Make sure it is in a place that is convenient.

2. Do you forget appointments a lot or show up late for things? Then maybe you should reconsider school counseling. If you are not the most reliable person, it might help if you have someone who comes to you. This is one of the great benefits of school counseling. In many clinics, if you have a pattern of being late for appointments or missing appointments, the counselor might not want to continue seeing you.

## Individual Counseling

Since you are a teenager, it is likely that counseling will take the form of one-on-one counseling. Most counselors will want to meet with a parent or guardian at least once to get your parent's or guardian's impression of what is going on as well as family medical history. After the initial visit, you will usually meet with your counselor for about fifty minutes. During this time, you can talk about whatever you want! This is a great way to get things off your chest and to also learn how to deal with anxiety-provoking situations.

## Group Counseling

Group counseling can be really helpful. It might sound kind of awful to you, or totally not be what you were thinking. Either way, it is worth giving it a shot. Groups are often made up of people dealing with similar issues (anxiety!) and people of similar age (teenagers!). Usually, you meet with the group leaders alone or with a parent or guardian prior to joining the group. During this session, the counselor will tell you what the group is about and see if you might be a good fit for the group and if the group is a good fit for you. Once you join the group, you will find that many of the discussions are initiated by the group leaders, but then it is left up to the group members to continue. You may find that suggestions given by other group members on how to cope with anxiety are better than the suggestions given by your leaders. Being around people your age who are experiencing similar stuff can make you feel a lot less isolated and reduce anxiety just by helping you realize that you are not alone.

Some things to think about with group counseling:

1. Do you have social anxiety or agoraphobia that is not manageable? If so, you might not be ready for a group. Starting off with some individual sessions in order to learn some coping skills could help you ease into a group.
2. Are you wary of sharing your fears? Joining a group for the first time might feel overwhelming. The idea of other people knowing your business could be a total turnoff. Group members tend to be pretty respectful of one another, though, so don't immediately decide against it!

## Family Counseling

Yikes! Who wants to do that? Well, if your family is the source of your anxiety and it's unlikely to get better unless there are some changes made around the house, family counseling may be just the type for you. In family counseling, sometimes there is just one counselor and sometimes there are two. In certain cases, the counselors might come to your house to see you and help intervene by observing what goes on at home that is making your anxiety difficult to handle. In an office, a counselor can still observe family dynamics and see how everyone around you manages, adds to, or helps you with your anxiety. This can be very helpful. Certain members of your family may be creating more anxiety for you, and neither you nor your family members would notice without the help of an outsider pointing it out.

Some things to consider with family therapy:

1. Is there any danger in bringing adults in your life to counseling? Is there a history of domestic violence or abuse that could be exacerbated by going to family counseling?
2. Is your family willing to listen and help? At first they might not be, so have patience and see if they change their tune

## Types of Counselors

Is the person you're seeing an MSW, LICSW, LMHC, LMFT, PhD, PsyD, EdD, MD, RNCNS, or PMHNP?

In all honesty, the letters after your counselor's name are important and indicate how much and what kind of education he or she has completed; however, the most important thing to think about when choosing a counselor is whether she is someone you feel you can talk with comfortably and who will listen to you. But you might as well know what all those letters mean! Also, depending on your state, the letters might vary a bit. For example, a PMHNP might be abbreviated to NP or PNP. You can always go to your state's licensing board website to find out which initials mean what!

- A person who has an MSW—master's degree in social work—has completed a two-year master's degree in social work.
- An LICSW—licensed independent clinical social worker—is an MSW who has completed two years of supervised post-degree clinical work and passed a state licensing exam.

- An LMHC—licensed mental health worker—has completed a two-year master's degree in mental health counseling, two years of supervised post-degree clinical work, and passed a state licensing exam.
- An LMFT—licensed marriage and family therapist—has completed a two-year master's degree in counseling and two years of supervised post-degree clinical work and passed a marriage and family therapy exam.
- A PhD has a doctor of philosophy degree.
- PsyD stands for doctor of psychology.
- EdD means doctor of education.

PhD, PsyD, and EdD degrees require completion of a doctoral program (some take five years), a clinical internship, and a residency, and then the person must pass a state licensing exam. These folks can do different types of assessments that many master's-level clinicians are not qualified to perform.

- An MD—medical doctor/psychiatrist—has completed medical school and, if he is seeing you for anxiety, should be a psychiatrist. To become psychiatrists, medical doctors must complete a three- to five-year postgraduate training program in psychiatry and successfully pass tests following the completion of their training. MDs can see patients for counseling as well as prescribe medications.
- PMHNPs—psychiatric mental health nurse practitioners—must have a master's degree from a psychiatric nurse practitioners program. They must also pass a state exam. NPs can prescribe medications as well as see patients in counseling.
- An RNCNS—clinical nurse specialist—is similar to the PMHNP. A clinical nurse specialist is a nurse who has gone on to further education in mental health. These nurses can prescribe medications as well as see patients for counseling.

## Questions to Ask:

1. I see you are an LMHC [or whatever letters the person has after his or her name]. What exactly does that mean?
2. Do you have experience working with people who have anxiety?
3. Do you have experience working with teenagers?

4. How often will I see you?
5. What is your deal with confidentiality? When would you have to tell someone what I said to you?
6. What are you going to tell my parent or guardian?
7. What will you tell my school?
8. Who are you allowed to talk to about me?
9. Do you have an emergency policy? Like if I freak out after hours, can I call you?
10. How long will each meeting last?
11. What is your cancellation policy?
12. What if I am not comfortable talking about something?
13. Will I be in counseling forever?
14. What happens when I am not anxious anymore? Do I still see you?

You can add your own questions too. Your parent or guardian may have questions about insurance, cost, cancellation policies, and confidentiality. It can be tough for a parent or guardian to let someone he doesn't know talk to his daughter about "stuff" without his knowing what is going on. So it is pretty normal for the adult in your life to be a little anxious signing you up for something like counseling.

After your questions have been answered, decide whether this person might be a good fit for you. It can take a few weeks to warm up to someone new, so give it a fair chance!

# Chapter 34

## Alternative Therapies

We are going to go over a few of the more popular alternative therapies that can be quite helpful when dealing with anxiety. The name alone, "alternative therapy," can sound a bit kooky, but these treatments or therapies have been around for years, and have proved time and again that they are quite successful for many people. Most important, you need to be comfortable with whatever treatment you are willing to try. If all of these sound a bit too weird for you at first, consider talking to practitioners in your area and asking all the questions you have on your mind before trying a treatment. Many practitioners have clients who will also be willing to talk to you about how they found treatment helpful. Keep in mind, however, if it doesn't feel right to you, maybe it *isn't* right for you. There are plenty of other options, so keep trying until you find something that works for you.

Once you do find something you would like to try, tune into your body to see how it feels before, during, immediately after, and a day after your treatment. At first you might not see a difference, but the next day you could wake up feeling a little less stressed or a little more refreshed. These treatments tend to take a bit of time to work, so don't expect an immediate fix. Look for subtle differences each time you go.

### Reiki

Reiki, according to the website www.reiki.org/faq/WhatIsReiki.html, is "a Japanese technique for stress reduction and relaxation that also promotes healing. It is administered by 'laying on hands' and is based on the idea that an unseen 'life force energy' flows through us and is what causes us to be alive. If one's 'life force energy' is low, then we are more likely to get sick or feel stress, and if it is high, we are more capable of being happy and healthy."

Reiki can be a little weird when you first try it; usually, the Reiki practitioner will put her hands on your head and you will feel this incredible warmth come from her hands—totally weird, right? Yes! But if you can yield to it, and enjoy the warmth, you could feel quite relaxed. The practitioner will move her hands to different areas of your body that she senses may need more energy.

## Massage

Massage, as defined by the American Massage Therapy Association (AMTA), is "a manual soft tissue manipulation, and includes holding, causing movement, and/or applying pressure to the body." The AMTA is one of three of the larger associations to which many massage therapists belong. The others are Associated Bodywork and Massage Professionals (ABMP) and the International Massage Association (IMA). There are many different types of massage; some are more intense than others. On the AMTA's website (www .amtamassage.org/about/terms.html), you can find definitions of the different types of massage as well as other massage terms. Massage is a great way to relieve stress as long as you don't mind being touched. Seriously, as soothing as massage can be for many, if you don't like anyone's hands on you, it probably isn't for you at this time. But, if you find you hold your tension in your muscles—like have a tight back, neck, jaw, or even feet—massage may be really helpful.

## Acupuncture

Acupuncture usually makes people cringe if they don't know much about it—needles sticking into me? NO WAY. First of all, the needles are so thin you hardly feel them. Second of all, acupuncturists can also do treatments that don't involve needles, so don't run away screaming just yet! The idea behind acupuncture is that our bodies have energy pathways within them that are known as meridians. If our meridians are blocked for any reason, it means that the energy within our bodies can't get to where it needs to be and we become out of balance. To correct the balance and the flow of energy in our bodies, acupuncturists use methods such as needles to unblock our pathways. It is pretty cool to think of our bodies as highways of energy! So, give it a try!

## Yoga Therapy

Yoga therapy is different from regular yoga. In yoga therapy, you meet one-on-one with a practitioner and are led through a meditation and yoga postures to help you connect to yourself on a deeper level. The teacher will often help you get into certain postures; this is another hands-on practice. The Phoenix Rising Yoga Therapy website, www.pryt.com, explains a yoga therapy session as "a one-on-one process lasting one-and-a-half hours. Through assisted yoga postures and non-directive dialogue, practitioners guide clients to experience the connection of their physical and emotional selves. Using focused breathing, this connection is held and explored, fostering release, personal growth and healing."

Some yoga therapists are only certified in yoga therapy, while others have a clinical mental health background. If you would like someone with a clinical background as well as a yoga background, be sure to check the credentials of people in your area.

If sitting still is tough for you and you like to move around, yoga therapy might be just the one for you to try. Reiki, massage, and acupuncture require more stillness in body than yoga therapy, so keep that in mind if you are someone who likes to move!

## Where Can I Find a Practitioner?

To find any of these practitioners, it can be helpful to ask your primary care physician. Many doctors' offices are offering alternative treatments or at least have lists of alternative practitioners that are known to be reputable in the area.

## Reiki

**http://iarp.org.** This is the website for the International Association of Reiki Professionals. It has a link that allows you to type in your zip code and pull up a list of registered professionals in your area.

## Massage

**www.amtamassage.org.** This is the American Massage Therapy Association's website. Also included on this website are listings of massage therapy schools. For a fraction of the price of a regular massage, you can obtain a massage from a massage therapy student at many of these schools.

**www.abmp.com/home.** This is the Associated Bodywork and Massage Professionals website, which also has information on massage and massage therapy schools.

**www.imagroup.com.** The International Massage Association website also has a great finder tool for massage therapists around the country.

## Acupuncture

**www.aaaomonline.org.** The website for the American Association of Acupuncture and Oriental Medicine has links to help you find a practitioner in your area as well as interesting information about acupuncture.

**www.medicalacupuncture.org.** This site is for the American Academy of Medical Acupuncturists. Practitioners found on this website are both physicians and acupuncturists.

## Yoga Therapy

**www.pryt.com/directory/directory.html.** This section of the Phoenix Rising Yoga Therapy website can link you to practitioners throughout the country.

**www.iayt.org.** This website is for the International Association of Yoga Therapists, and it has a section to help link you to a yoga therapist in your area as well as interesting research done on yoga therapy.

### General and Helpful Information

The National Institutes of Health have a web page for the National Center for Complementary and Alternative Medicine. Their main website, http://nccam.nih.gov, has links to research and cool information.

Although they will not help you link to providers, there is a portion of their website that has a great list of questions to ask potential providers and what to look for in a provider. Go to http://nccam.nih.gov/health/decisions/ practitioner.htm.

State licensing boards are a great place to check whether the practitioner you are interested in has the appropriate license to practice in your state. You can access licensing boards on the Internet by searching for your state name along with "licensing board."

# Chapter 35

## Medication

In some cases, anxiety can be so overwhelming for you that your health-care provider may feel it is time to try some medicine. The idea of taking medication really freaks out some people. Of course, many of us would take medicine if we had strep throat or some other physical ailment, but taking something for mental health reasons can often feel funny. Well, try to think of mental health just like your physical health. After all, they are intertwined, and both your mind and body need to be healthy so that you can be at your best. Also, keep in mind that just because you might need to take medication now, it does not mean that you will have to take it forever. Maybe you need the help of some medicine while you work on other methods of dealing with your anxiety, such as the activities and exercises described in this book. Maybe you are going through an especially anxious time in your life. There is nothing wrong with taking medication as prescribed by your doctor if it is going to help you feel better.

### What Are the Most Popular Medications for Anxiety in Teenagers?

According to the Anxiety Disorders Association of America's website (www .adaa.org), most doctors will prescribe a class of medications known as SSRIs—selective serotonin reuptake inhibitors. The name is a mouthful, but the quick explanation is that this medication helps your brain regulate the amount of serotonin your body produces. Without enough serotonin, people can feel depressed and often anxious. There are many different SSRIs: fluox-etine (Prozac), sertraline (Zoloft), paroxetine (Paxil), fluvoxamine (Luvox), citalopram (Celexa), and escitalopram (Lexapro) are the most common, and the ones you may have heard about already. The first word is the generic name, and the capitalized word in parentheses is the brand name, which also happens to be the name you will usually see in television commercials. SSRIs can be very helpful; however, they do take time to work. You won't feel a difference the first time you take it. You often need to give the medicine about four weeks until it is in your system enough to make a difference.

Another class of medications prescribed for anxiety is the benzodiazepines—another mouthful! These medicines are not the first choice for many doctors because they can be very addictive. Some of the more common benzodiazepines are alprazolam (Xanax), lorazepam (Ativan), diazepam (Valium), clonazepam (Klonopin). These work differently than the SSRIs.

## Important Things to Know

If you do end up taking any medications for anything, it is extremely important to communicate with your health-care provider and parent or guardian. Medicines, even the best ones, can have side effects, and since everyone's body is different, you may end up with side effects or you may not. Your health-care provider can warn you about potential side effects, but he or she cannot predict whether you will actually experience any. This is why it is important to communicate with the adults involved in your treatment. If you are having side effects, talk to those involved and let them know what you are feeling. Sometimes adjustments can be made that are as easy as changing the amount of medicine you are taking, the time you are taking it, or perhaps trying a new medication.

The best way for you to get the best treatment you need is to advocate for yourself when you are with your health-care provider. This can seem intimidating, but remember, this is your body; you have the right to know what is going in it and why. Not sure what to say to your health-care provider? Consider using the following questions to express your concerns and find out what you are taking and why.

### Questions for Your Health-Care Provider

1. Why do you think this medication in particular will help me?
2. What are the most common side effects of this medicine?
3. Will the side effects go away after a period of time?

4.  Is there anything I shouldn't do while taking this medication (foods not to eat, activities to be careful with, other medications that might interact)?
5.  How long will it take for me to tell if this is working or not?
6.  Is this medication addictive?
7.  Is there a better time of day to take the medicine?
8.  Should I take it with food or without?
9.  Am I going to be on this forever?
10. What if I don't like it?
11. What happens if I forget to take it one day?
12. Is there anything I can do along with this medicine that might help with my anxiety?

# Acknowledgments

I would like to thank my wonderful family and friends for helping me write this book. Without their support, refusal to speak to me when I was procrastinating, and late-night texts telling me I could do it, I would never have gotten through all of this. I also must thank my agent, editor, mentor, supercool friend, Janice Pieroni of Story Arts Management for always supporting me and cheering me on, and definitely helping to reduce my anxiety. Steve Deger at Fairview Press for being cool and down to earth and totally appreciating my voice. Mary Byers for enjoying grammar as much as me, myself, and I. Nicole Maniez, acupuncturist extraordinaire, who really reduced my stress when I needed it most. My high school guidance counselor Tony King and my English professor Helen Whall at Holy Cross, without whom I would never have dealt with my own anxiety or had the self-esteem to keep following my dreams (THANK YOU THANK YOU THANK YOU).

And last but not least my husband, who not only had to deal with my anxiety over meeting my deadline, but also had to deal with my deadline for this book coinciding—to the day—with my due date. Thank you, Gavin, for making me so uncomfortable in those last months that I was not able to sleep and therefore had to spend time writing all night long, and also for being the best reward ever for finishing on time!